Praise for **F the Shoulds. Do the Wants.**

'F the Shoulds. Do the Wants. *is like Windex for the soul. Pick this book up anytime you need to remember what really matters.'*

Kathryn Budig, author of *Aim True* and founder of Haus of Phoenix

'As *I always say, SHOULD IS AN ASSHOLE, and Tricia Huffman's is the voice you want in your ear to teach you how to stop shoulding on yourself. She's effortlessly wise, spit-out-your-coffee funny, and most of all, she's authentic. She tells it as it is, but in such a way that we don't ever lose hope. She's the real deal.'*

Jennifer Pastiloff, bestselling author of *On Being Human*

'F the Shoulds. Do the Wants. *reveals how much of our lives have been constructed based on how our choices look to others instead of how they feel to us. By sharing raw, personal stories of uncovering the deep-rooted shoulds in her own life, Tricia gifts us a powerful tool in self-awareness—constantly guiding us back to asking, "What do I really* **want**?"'

Amber Rae, bestselling author of *Choose Wonder Over Worry* and *The Answers Are Within You*

'Tricia *is one of the most inspiring, open-hearted souls I know. She's the guide you need when you're seeking freedom from your excuses and self-doubt. If you're ready to step into your full, joyous self and be the person you're meant to be, let Tricia lead you the way there!'*

Cathy Heller, top podcast host, business coach and bestselling author of *Don't Keep Your Day Job*

'Tricia *is that no-nonsense best friend that you want on your A-team to make sure you don't travel down the tunnel of despair and stay there. Her simple and fun approach is easy to follow and make a part of well-being rituals.'*

Koya Webb, author of *Let Your Fears Make You Fierce*

'In *a world that's constantly demanding so much from us, it can feel easy to lose yourself and feel disconnected from your passions. Tricia has a down-to-earth and compassionate way to help us reclaim our lives.'*

— **Jessica Ortner**, *New York Times* bestselling author

'F the Shoulds. Do the Wants. *is filled with practical advice and strategies to get out of your own way to liberate yourself from regrets so you can create the happy, healthy life you deserve. Tricia Huffman has created a powerful resource guide that includes big and small steps that anyone can take to stay firmly planted in the present while learning from the past. Tricia is an inspiring, wise, and compassionate teacher who leads with truth, humor, and self-kindness.'*

Terri Cole, psychotherapist and author of *Boundary Boss*

'Tricia is delivering a really powerful concept that slows down our process and lets us look at what is motivating our behavior. It is an incredibly powerful life hack.'

Dan Peres, award-winning editor-in-chief of *Details* and author of *As Needed for Pain*

'Tricia has a way of writing that feels reminiscent of checking in with an old friend. In this book, she reminds you that you and only you are in control of your one sweet, precious life, so why the f@$% aren't you doing what YOU **want***? It woke me up to seeing that if you aren't being present and doing what you* **want** *with your life—what are you even doing?* F the Shoulds. Do the Wants. *will inspire you to remember who you are and what you* **want** *and gently nudge you to recognize where the shoulds are running your life as it gives you the courage to start living in accordance to your true* **wants***, dreams, and desires.'*

Tristan Prettyman, singer-songwriter

'This Carrie Bradshaw quote from an episode of Sex and the City *is something that has always stuck with me: 'I wondered if should was another disease plaguing women . . . Why are we should-ing all over ourselves?'* F the Shoulds. Do the Wants. *exposes the varied ways that the shoulds are plaguing not just women, but everyone. Tricia powerfully, yet compassionately, shows how to get clear on what is weighing on you and the shoulds that are holding you back and keeping you from trusting your gut and who you are. Her work with shifting away from shoulds and into* **wants** *gets us to living out the true joy of who we are.'*

Robyn Youkilis, two-time bestselling author, wellness coach and influencer

'In a world where so many are seeking a deeper connection to themselves, their purpose and to their own worth, Tricia guides us to this simple yet powerful concept showing us that by reframing our word choice we are reframing our relationship to ourselves and our lives.'

Karen Salmansohn, bestselling author of *Think Happy*

F THE SHOULDS.
DO THE WANTS.

F THE SHOULDS. DO THE WANTS.

Get Clear on Who You Are, What You Want and Why You Want It.

Tricia Huffman

HAY HOUSE

Carlsbad, California • New York City
London • Sydney • New Delhi

Published in the United Kingdom by:
Hay House UK Ltd, The Sixth Floor, Watson House,
54 Baker Street, London W1U 7BU
Tel: +44 (0)20 3927 7290; Fax: +44 (0)20 3927 7291; www.hayhouse.co.uk

Published in the United States of America by:
Hay House Inc., PO Box 5100, Carlsbad, CA 92018-5100
Tel: (1) 760 431 7695 or (800) 654 5126
Fax: (1) 760 431 6948 or (800) 650 5115; www.hayhouse.com

Published in Australia by:
Hay House Australia Ltd, 18/36 Ralph St, Alexandria NSW 2015
Tel: (61) 2 9669 4299; Fax: (61) 2 9669 4144; www.hayhouse.com.au

Published in India by:
Hay House Publishers India, Muskaan Complex, Plot No.3, B-2,
Vasant Kunj, New Delhi 110 070
Tel: (91) 11 4176 1620; Fax: (91) 11 4176 1630; www.hayhouse.co.in

Text © Tricia Huffman, 2022

Project editor: Melody Guy
Cover design: Kathleen Lynch
Interior design: Greg Johnson, Textbook Perfect

A catalogue record for this book is available from the British Library.

Tradepaper ISBN: 978-1-78817-675-0
E-book ISBN: 978-1-4019-6439-9
Audiobook ISBN: 978-1-4019-6440-5

Printed and bound by CPI Group (UK) Ltd, Croydon CR0 4YY

I wrote this book for you.
Yes, you.
I truly hope it empowers you
to F the shoulds and do your wants
in the tiny ways
and the huge ways.
This life is yours.
Don't ever forget that, okay?

CONTENTS

FOREWORD

I've always considered myself a dreamer—and I've always been foolish enough to think my dreams can and will come true. This naïveté has worked out to my benefit over and over again: in music, philanthropy, investments, and even relationships. Plan B never appeals to me, and I always hustle to re-imagine Plan A when I need to. But I wasn't always experienced in the art of courageously leaping before the net appeared. That skill began to crystallize during my experimental and uncertain college years.

I went to school for musical theatre. It was an easy choice. I like to entertain and I wanted to be singing on a stage. My school was in Manhattan—a dream environment for any artist. Perhaps it was the city, or the sense of freedom that comes with being 18, that led me to connect deeply with songwriting as soon as I arrived at college. For me, songwriting paired personal journaling with my lifelong joy of singing. On many occasions, I wouldn't even have time to write my songs down—I'd just make them up, freestyling on prompts to the delight of my friends and neighbors. Something inside of me knew how to do it. The more I practiced, the better I got. My song catalog grew quickly. Seeing these results unfold convinced me I could go far if I wanted—and I wanted!

I was only two semesters into college when I decided the experience was unfulfilling. My passion was creating original music and performing it live. My school only offered ways to perform pre-existing material and learn how to audition. I wanted to skip the auditions and get right to the good stuff. I constantly asked myself, "Should I pursue my music? Should I drop out of college?" Answering *yes* to either of those questions seemed obvious to me, but it felt more terrifying than exhilarating. I wanted someone or something outside of myself to tell me YES! Go! I wanted direction or at least some confirmation from my peers and parents, but I wasn't getting it. Until…

On a fateful day in Sheep Meadow, a vast green lawn in Central Park and playground for city sunseekers and Frisbee throwers, a stranger approached. He was a middle-aged, long-haired mystic dressed in flowing, loose clothing, working the crowds to help remove the spells and sour faces that a city like New York can easily cast. He grabbed my hand, turned my palm upward, studying my hand with a magician's flair and a curious gaze. Then he said the magic words that helped steer my life onto its destined course. "Youth!" he said, staring seriously at my baby face. "Avoid the questioner and go with what you know." And in that moment, all the sounds of the city faded away. It was a cosmic mic drop. Yes! Stop asking questions! I already know the answer.

His words still echo today in the pages of *F the Shoulds. Do the Wants.* This is why I love Tricia Huffman and her mission to remove *should* from our vocabulary. Tricia is not the palm reader in my story, but she came into my life just as serendipitously and continues to inspire me with her practical magic.

Thanks to the good fortune of meeting the palm reader on that fateful day in 1996, I immediately dropped out of college to pursue original music. That also meant accepting the repercussions: the reality of being broke and needing to work odd jobs along the way.

Just up the street from my apartment was a big bookstore. A friend in my building worked there and pulled some strings to get me an interview. I made up a story about working at my high school library, and I got the job. I didn't know what I was getting myself into; I just needed rent money. Yet, claiming my joy and following my heart led me right where I was meant to begin my journey. At the bookstore I was instructed to learn the authors and subjects in both the Rock 'n' Roll and New Age sections. Funny how those two subjects were right next to each other; Zappa and Ziggy Stardust dovetailed right into *The Artist's Way* and Astrology. This bookstore job suddenly offered views greater than those overlooking Broadway—windows into worlds of musical success as well as meditations for mindfulness and self-realization.

This intersection of books would become a guidepost for my personal life and career, taking me down a path to joy, gratitude, and abundance. This job I landed (because it was the next necessary step in following my heart) gifted me a wealth of resources—tools for sustained happiness and a multitude of successes. Much of the medicine I pour into my music is gleaned from a garden of self-help books.

This book by my friend Tricia Huffman is up there with the best of them. Thoughtfully compiled with personal stories, some evolved from her podcast interviews and Tricia's own discoveries and distinctions earned from years of inquiry, *F the Shoulds. Do the Wants.* is designed to challenge us to rethink our words and reshape our thoughts in subtle ways that help remove unwanted doubt, guilt, and delay.

A dream can be fulfilled today. What *are* we waiting for? If you're waiting for your palm reader to find you and tell you it's okay to go for it—congratulations, you've just been introduced to Tricia Huffman and it's time to claim your joy.

Tricia came into my life through the music industry when she was hired to be my monitor engineer, the sound technician on the side of the stage who mixes the playback for the band to hear. She is a gifted and talented audio engineer who rose to the top in her field, but she still remarkably wanted to pursue something higher and more personal for the benefit of others. Just like my job at the bookstore, she stands at the intersection of Rock 'n' Roll and New Age—a paradox of loud and sensitive; confronting yet comforting; edgy as a roadie yet tender as a new mama.

As my musical career was taking off, I was lucky to have Tricia in the wings to help keep my head on my shoulders and my feet on the ground. For reasons she will explain, she flipped the definition of sound technician to that of someone who pushes the right buttons to dial in mindfulness and joy. A *sound* technician. On the road she coached mindfulness and accountability for all the opportunities, appointments, and promises I was making. She was my "manager of integrity." Today, she provides a similar service in this book—and as Your Joyologist—on a mission to see you claim joy in your daily life.

I believe a book finds us right when we need it the most. We open it and it consumes us when we're ready to receive its offering. I won't say you *should* read this because that goes against everything the book is about. You will read this when you want to—and with each anecdote, idea, and distinction, you will gain victory over your questioner and ultimately go with what you know.

Enjoy!

In joy,
JASON MRAZ
Singer/Songwriter
Oceanside, CA, 2021

INTRODUCTION

I had a generally good childhood—basic, midwestern, suburban. My parents worked hard to provide for us so that we could have the things they thought we *should* have. We lived in a split-level, three-bedroom home with a big yard and a pool. My dad leased a brand-new Infiniti when they first came out, even though we couldn't afford it, because he wanted to look a certain way to the outside world and himself. My mom was a nurse who took on extra jobs like collecting plasma at night after her day shift at the surgery center so that we could have Nike sneakers, Barbies, cable TV, and take vacations. We had everything that we needed—more than we needed—yet it always felt like we were struggling. Like we were stuck behind some invisible not-enough gate. It felt like there was this pressure that we *should* have more, that we *should* be more, that we didn't have enough, that we weren't enough.

In school, I was very aware of the desire to fit in. I felt and noticed in others this hesitation before naming a favorite show, song, and more. We were afraid of saying the wrong thing and being made fun of. It was as if we needed approval on what we *should* like, want, be. I saw all the teasing and the nonsensical reasons that kids chose to pick on others and exclude them. I felt the inner battle of: *Should I raise my hand and speak up? Or is it not cool to participate? Will people think that I am smart or a Goody Two-Shoes if I raise my hand? I shouldn't be seen talking to Kim because Katie says she is a nerd, so I don't want everyone to think that I am a nerd and be made fun of too. But I like Kim; she's funny.* I should *have a boyfriend.* Then *people will think of me as cool, interesting, and worthy of hanging out with. Why don't boys like me? What can I do to make boys like me? Ugh*, everything felt so hard and confusing.

I was so fed up with navigating what I *should* and *should* not do, never feeling like I was making the "right" choices and always looking around to see if I had. *Do you like me? Is what I am wearing good enough? Is what I just said funny?* I was always searching for the validation that I was worthy, that I was cool enough, smart enough, interesting enough, attractive enough, and on and on. I would get a taste of it (they like me!), and then feel like I was chasing their approval all over again. **That is what happens when you are always looking outside of yourself for validation: you will always be chasing it, no matter how much you get.**

By the time I reached 15 years old, I was miserable, even though I had loads of friends, got good grades without trying too hard, and could be labeled as "popular." Externally, I had a lot, but I felt so alone. Misunderstood. Like no one truly cared about me, knew me, or saw the real me. I wanted both to fit in and stand out. I was self-confident yet always looking outside of myself for confirmation that what I was doing and saying was acceptable. That who I was, was acceptable. I wanted to feel accepted. I wanted to feel admired. I wanted to feel seen. I wanted to feel loved. And no matter what I did, it never felt like I was enough.

Life felt overwhelming to me, and I just didn't understand the point of living this way with all of these made-up rules of what we *should* look like, act like, what music we *should* like, what trends we *should* follow, what career paths we *should* take, etc. Especially when I rarely saw adults who were truly enjoying and living their lives instead of just going through the motions. I mean, what was the freaking point of being alive just to play follow-the-leader while always comparing yourself to others, feeling terrible about yourself, and worrying that you weren't doing it right, whatever "it" was?

I also happened to have undiagnosed chronic pain, exhaustion, and digestion issues, which would later be diagnosed as fibromyalgia. There was a benefit to living with all of these physical challenges, though. I believe they gave me a greater bullshit detector. I was in so much physical pain that I could not also handle the daily emotional pain we as humans create for ourselves.

One day, I had a complete breakdown—a locked-in-the-bathroom-all-day, drawing-on-the-mirror-in-red-lipstick kind of breakdown during which I gave myself two choices. I could go through with my plan to end my life by taking all my dad's sleeping medication, *or* I could try life a different way.

What if I fully chose to live *my life*? What if instead of putting so much attention on what other people thought of me, I put my attention on what *I* thought about me? What if I did what I wanted, what felt best to me, and made my own opinion be the most important one in my mind and in my heart? What if I focused more energy on accepting myself and less energy looking for others to accept me?

It was a wake-up call that showed me that, while I couldn't do much about the physical pain, I could do something about the emotional pain that I was living in and creating for myself. My physical pain was a real burden, but I was also carrying so much weight from the relentless craving to be accepted. I saw that I wasn't fully allowing myself to be myself, to honor myself, and to actually share my true self with others.

In that moment, I chose to live.

I remember turning on the water as hot as it would go and sobbing in the shower until there were no more tears to shed and my skin had turned red. I don't recommend this, and I don't know how I did it. It wasn't a plan; it just happened. Something transpired in that shower. It was like I was burning away all the heaviness of worrying about other people's thoughts, opinions, and judgments. I was setting myself free.

That day, that choice, was monumental. From then on, I leaned in to what I now know was my intuition. I did, said, and wore what felt right and true to me, regardless of the fear of being judged by others. I committed to myself. I committed to listening to myself and trusting myself over what anyone else thought, including my parents, my friends, my counselors, my teachers, the cool kids—anyone and everyone. I stood up for myself and others and believed that I was capable of making my dreams come true, even if I didn't know how, because I wanted to *live* my life. I did me, even when it felt like no one else supported me or saw me. It wasn't easy (it still isn't), but I knew that day in the shower that I wasn't just making a choice for that moment, but that it would take me recommitting to myself and to living *my* life daily.

So, you see, I am the *last* person that I would have labeled as someone who lived a life of *shoulds.* If you had asked family members, co-workers, and friends, they would have said the same. Tricia? She does what she *wants.* She *lives her* life her way, all the way. I did. I have lived a freaking awesome life!

I did *not* think that I lived a life run by *shoulds,* and you may think that you don't either. But later in life (we will get to that story next), when I decided to completely ban that one word from my life, I couldn't have predicted the impact that it would have on me. I had no clue how much would be revealed to me and how truly transformational the journey would still be to this day just by removing that one word from my vocabulary.

And that is what I want for you too.

I am going to guide you to uncover and kick the F'ing *shoulds* out of your life for good so that you can actually live a life that is true to *you.* So that every day you can claim your worth, your joy, your life! I will prove to you that this is not a selfish pursuit and that living your *wants* is not only for your best but for the best of everyone you come into contact with. In this book, we are going to go *deep,* because that is what the *shoulds* do—they dig into us so deeply that we don't even know that they are there.

The first question I want you to consider is:

Are your **wants** actually your own, or have you been influenced to believe you *should* **want** them?

We are going to find that out and so much more! Let's dive in!

CHAPTER 1

F THE *SHOULDS.*

At the age of 27, I was touring the world with Grammy Award–winning icons. As their sound monitor engineer, I was in charge of what they heard on stage. The audio for each microphone and instrument went through my sound console, and then I controlled a "mix" for each person on stage of their own microphone, instruments, and everyone else's so that they could perform their best each night. It was incredibly fulfilling and exciting work. I was living my dream and I loved it. And then one day, as I was preparing to leave on a red-eye to Australia for a world tour with Jason Mraz, I got the shocking news that my father had been found dead in his car. In that moment, my life and my way of living changed forever.

I flew from California to Ohio for the funeral, but the next day I was back on another plane, heading to Australia to keep working. Honestly, I didn't know what else to do, and my work family felt more like home than my blood family at the time. I did what so many of us feel we *should* do when tragedy strikes and we don't know what else to do: just keep going through the motions of life. But on tour, I was a mess. It was like I had been cracked open and everywhere I went, I couldn't help but notice all the people at airports, in line at restaurants, and wandering sidewalks around the world looking miserable, unhappy, and unfulfilled.

Every time I saw these people, I thought of my father. While getting into his car, he had slipped on a patch of ice and hit his head. He made it into his car but passed out from the head injury and was found dead the next day. His cause of death was hypothermia. I mean, what the actual fuck! You can slip on a patch of ice and that's it. Your life is done. All of those things you had been putting off until later. All of those wants that you never allowed yourself to pursue. All of it is gone. I wanted to shake the people I passed on the street and yell, "Wake up! You could die tomorrow! You really don't know! Live your life! Enjoy it, instead of making it even harder for yourself! Stop holding yourself back. Do what *you* want to do! Say the things that you want to say. Be who you want to be. Stop just going through the motions and following the *shoulds*. Be alive while you are still living!"

After a few weeks on the road, sobbing behind my sound console, I made the hard call to quit my dream job and leave my favorite touring family behind, along with two prebooked years of traveling the world and the hefty income that would have come with it. I had absolutely no clue what I was going to do or where I would go. I didn't even really have a place to live because I was always on tour or traveling on my own. The only thing I did know was that I was done with the *shoulds* and that I wanted to shake people up and guide them to live their own lives while they still had one.

When my father passed away, I was overcome with this strong internal message to completely eliminate the word *should* from my life. Not just the idea of not living the *shoulds,* or "shoulding on myself," but to take it one step further and *fully kick the word out of my life.* I have no idea where this message came from. I don't remember anyone telling me to do it or reading about not using the word *should*—I just knew that I was done with it. And when I said, "done with that word," I meant it. I literally would not let the word come out of my mouth. Mid-sentence, mid-word, I would realize I was about to say *should* and would stand there stuttering, looking for another word to replace it. I had absolutely no idea how much *shoulds* were running my life when I took on this quest. I mean, me? The kickass female sound engineer who was constantly pushing limitations and boundaries? I did not live a life of *shoulds!* I believed that I followed my own internal compass. I did what I wanted and *loved* my life!

Yet, right away, by committing to this one-word elimination, I started to see how my life had been ruled in big and small ways by thoughts of what I thought I *should* do and who I *should* be. I would catch myself saying things like: "I *shouldn't* eat pizza" (even a healthified, gluten-free, and vegan version) and then feel guilt and shame when I said F it and did. "I *should* be able to fit into a size medium" and then be mad at myself for the way my body naturally was because I wasn't being "good" enough at being fit and healthy. I *should* wear this dress more often because I spent a lot of money on it, even though I really don't love how it looks on me. I *should* be able to get into a freestanding handstand by now (I mean, I have been practicing yoga for years). I *should* go meet my friends at the bar because I have been feeling lonely, even though I don't like bars. I *shouldn't* like this song; it's so cheesy. All day long this word was infiltrating my life and making me feel bad about myself.

It was astonishing to discover that regularly and mindlessly using *should* had contributed to me questioning my worth, keeping myself small, and muddying my intuition with doubts, fears, shame, comparisons, and internal judgments. That word made me feel like shit and robbed me of so much joy. It kept me from trusting myself and allowing myself to enjoy what I **wanted**. I saw how often I was defaulting to the shitty *shoulds* that had been programmed into me, and even in the times when I listened to myself and my **wants**, I would question my choices, start to compare my choices to other people's choices, and then fall into the *should haves*—I *should have* done this, I *shouldn't have* said that.

I know that I am not alone in the many ways that *should* had been holding me back. And just as I wanted to shout, "Wake up!" to everyone I saw on the street after my father's death, I am now (lovingly) shouting, "Wake up!" to you. The *shoulds* are shitty. The *shoulds* are heavy. The *shoulds* are manipulative.

They are holding you back in ways that you can't even imagine, and they are everywhere. Trust me, you won't know the fullness of what your life can be until you F the *shoulds* for good!

"The *shoulds* are shitty.
The *shoulds* are heavy.
The *shoulds* are
manipulative.
They are holding you back
in ways that you can't
even imagine,
and they are everywhere.
Trust me, you won't know
the fullness of what
your life can be until you
F the *shoulds* for good!"

LIVING THE *SHOULDS*

Resentment, doubt, fear, shame, guilt (that's quite the company). What do all of these fun emotions have in common? They are the result of living in the *shoulds*. *Shoulds* are at the root of so many of our icky, heavy-weighted emotions, and they breed anxiety, self-doubt, comparison, judgments, and more. From the minute we wake up to the minute we fall asleep, *shoulds* are constantly being pushed on us—by our own minds, the outside world, the media, marketing, and even by those who love us the most. The *shoulds* keep us from trusting ourselves, sending us the message that we are not enough and preventing us from living our lives to our truest capacity.

Shoulds are sneaky and deceptive. Even though I gave them up over 12 years ago, that doesn't mean that I am immune to them. There are still mornings that, as soon as I wake up, I can feel the *should* struggle. I reach for my phone and—bam!—get hit with:

I shouldn't look at my phone right away! Everyone says I should spend the first hour of my day unplugged. I should have woken up earlier. I should get up and do yoga. I should have lemon water. I should eat xyz healthy food trend for breakfast. I should have cleaned up the house better last night. I should be packing the kids' lunches with more variety. I should have packed their lunches last night (that's what every other mom I know does). I shouldn't compare myself to other moms. I should be grateful that I get to wake up and have these silly struggles.

And then I open my e-mails and social media and get even more *shoulds* directed at me. Why you *should* do breathwork. How you *should* parent your children. The conversations you *should* be having with your partner.

Why you *should* be intermittent fasting. You *should* make this recipe that Gwyneth Paltrow loves! How you *should* be investing your money.

And on and on and on. All. Day. Long.

The *shoulds* are nonstop! Did you start to feel a little overwhelmed by that slight glimpse into how often the *shoulds* can appear in just a few minutes of the day? I feel like I need to take a nap after typing that paragraph. We are inundated with *shoulds, even* from the people we look up to, the ones who are trying to empower us, the ones teaching us how to take care of and love ourselves. Self-care and self-love, anyone? These are major buzzwords for good reason. But promoting these things while *should-ing* the best self-care practices may actually lead to more feelings of guilt, shame, and overwhelm. Leaving people confused about how to take care of themselves and love themselves the "right" way, feeling less than or beating themselves up for not doing all the things, all the time. The way they *should* (insert vomit emoji here) be.

Yes, we must take care of ourselves. It is necessary to love and accept ourselves in order to live a life true to who we are and the ultimate act of self-care is to stop living a life of *shoulds*! I am serious! Imagine how exponentially your love and appreciation for your own self will grow when you stop *shoulding* all over yourself and actually start to listen to what you need and want instead of just following the lead of what others tell you that you *should* do! You are uniquely you and your life is uniquely yours. What works for someone else (even someone you look up to and who feels aligned with you) may not be for you, for your life, for your family, for your now. And that doesn't mean that anything is wrong with you or that there is anything wrong with them, or their advice and way of doing things. Once you begin to release the *shoulds*, you'll discover that you and only you are the authority in your life!

Shoulds are not going to magically disappear when you read this book. I already admitted I still often feel the weight of them. The *shoulds* of life and those that pop up in your mind may never totally go away, *but* once you become aware of all the *shoulds* coming at you each day, you will be able to reframe them and see that every time you see, feel, or think a *should*, you actually have a choice. You will start to see each *should* as a space to get curious and ask yourself questions. You will be empowered to look deeper and move beyond the *should*, and instead choose beliefs and behaviors that nurture and empower you and are more aligned with who you truly are and *want* to be. You will learn that each *should* is an opportunity for discovery and not a heavy, uncomfortable burden that you must carry or find a way to make work.

> Once you begin to release the *shoulds*, you'll discover that you and only you are the authority in your life. Once you become aware of all the *shoulds* coming at you each day, you will be able to reframe them and see that every time you see, feel, or think a *should*, you actually have a choice.

UNSHOULDING OURSELVES

I doubt any of us can remember learning the word *should*. I sure don't. But what I do know is that my four-year-old daughter uses it regularly and my two-year-old says it now too. This coming from two kids whose mother does not ever use the word! I even substitute another word for *should* when reading their books to them or any other place it is written. I am that committed.

Talk about a punch to the gut. While I am teaching them to not lean on that word, I can't ignore how deeply ingrained it is in our everyday internal and external dialogue. When my four-year-old says *should*, she likely (hopefully) doesn't feel any associated negativity, and yet I see her looking to me to give her the answer. Because as soon as she uses the word *should*, she begins to look outside of herself. As her mother, I gently nudge her to look within. Yes, she is four and wants her mother's direction and approval, *but* when she asks me things like, "What *should* I color, Momma?" I reply, "What do you want to color, Zia? What would feel fun for you to color?"

The words we choose have so much power over our internal understanding of ourselves and the world. And as a parent, I can see that she is already creating her sense of what is right and wrong based around *shoulds* and other people's reactions and validation. *She is already starting to acquire and wear the unconscious weight of the outside world's expectations—prioritizing the world's reflection of her over her own.* Every day these "little" things add up and start to chip away at us, diluting our connection to ourselves.

That is the impact the word *should* has on our lives and the choices we make—big and small—every day. When you are living in the *shoulds*, you are making the outside world's perception of you more important than your perception of you. You are making what you think everyone else—the world at large—wants and expects from you to be more important than what you want for yourself! If you are always, always leaning on *should*, how do you ever expect to learn the truth about yourself and what you truly feel and *want*?

While recording for my podcast, Meredith Atwood, author of *The Year of No Nonsense*, confessed that she had spent her whole life making decisions based on seeking validation from others. Now, at 40 years old, she is finally asking herself, What do *I want*? No matter your age, no matter your situation—you can free yourself from the *shoulds*. Honestly, how much more of this life do you want to spend being more concerned about what other people think of you than of what *you* think of you? How much more of your life do you want to spend living by an invisible set of rules that has you not trusting yourself, continuously abandoning yourself, always seeking validation outside of yourself, and that is robbing you of joy? Trust me, it is way more enlivening and fulfilling to F the *shoulds* than to blindly follow them.

And, by the way, we are always learning, growing, and evolving! You may be stuck or get stuck *shoulding* yourself into following through or sticking with what you wanted 10 years ago, 10 months ago, 10 days ago, even 10 minutes ago. You are allowed to change your mind and not feel you *should* stick with what you once thought you wanted or dreamed you would be. And you don't have to feel bad about that.

> You are allowed to change your mind and not feel you *should* stick with what you once thought you wanted or dreamed you would be. And you don't have to feel bad about that!

"When you are living in the *shoulds*, you are making the outside world's perception of you more important than your perception of you."

IT'S NOT JUST A SIX-LETTER WORD

I was 15 minutes into recording for my podcast with my friend Mona Tavakoli, a badass drummer, when I had to pause our conversation to bring her attention to her constant use of the word *should*. She has known me since I gave up the word and knows how I feel about it. So, she was shocked to hear that she had used the word at all, and committed to omitting it moving forward after hearing a little mini *should* thesis from me. Yet it kept spilling out of her mouth, again and again, despite her best efforts. I was laughing (not judging) as I kept pointing it out. She was awestruck as she suddenly woke up to how deeply ingrained the word was in her vernacular and therefore her life.

Before I evicted that word myself, it had been deep in my own vernacular too, and it's most likely super deep in yours. But here is the thing: sometimes you just don't know until you know! Because *shoulds* make what is right and wrong murky. They leave little room for you to consider and honor your own opinion. I want you to be able to make decisions for yourself and to consider the *whys* behind your choices, including what you do and what you do not **want**. Don't you want that for yourself too? When we start questioning the *shoulds*, we begin to realize how much we have been looking outside of ourselves for feedback, approval, and permission.

You could be thinking, *Calm down, lady:* should *is just a word.* Is this whole book really all about *shoulds*? Yes, yes it is. But also *no*—it is about *so* much more. Because *should* isn't just a word; it is a feeling. A feeling that infiltrates a lot of our lives including our beliefs about ourselves. *Shoulds* are often invisible, so even if you think that you don't use the word, or that it doesn't have power over you, you are likely still feeling and fighting the deep-rooted effects of *should*. This book will take you on a journey to expose the *shoulds* and the many ways they seep into your life and psyche, giving you the wisdom and power to eliminate them. By F'ing the *shoulds*, we get to come back home to ourselves over and over again.

Pause for a minute and try to imagine some of the ways that *should* shows up in your daily life. If you haven't been tuned in to this word and the energy of it, you may be sitting there like, uh, I don't know. Most of us are so used to that word driving our life choices and dialogue that we can't even see it! Allow me to name a few ways *should* may show up in your daily life:

- I *should* wake up earlier.
- I *should* go to bed earlier.
- What *should* I wear today?
- I *should* have gotten more done today.
- I *should* call my mom.
- What *should* I eat for dinner?
- I *should* be further along in my career.
- I *should* be saving more money.
- What *should* I do about _____?
- I *should* exercise today.
- I *shouldn't* have eaten that.
- *Should* I buy this or that?
- I *shouldn't* drink another coffee.
- I *shouldn't* feel this way when I know I have it so much better than others.

- What *should* I say to _____?
- I *shouldn't* have said that.

It's *everywhere*! Start to tune in to that word. Be aware of it in what you read and what you watch (even when you read from or talk to people you look up to). Notice when you say it; be aware of it in your thoughts and how it comes up throughout your day. Instead of just seeing it as a harmless six-letter word, see it as a poisonous dart that enters your bloodstream and starts to control your entire life, including what and how you feel about yourself.

So many people are so deep in the *shoulds* that they don't even know what they actually feel or believe about themselves. You may be so locked into the *shoulds* of life that you are not allowing yourself to see what is possible for you or to even ask yourself what it is that you truly **want**. Please, be gentle with yourself as you start to untangle yourself from the *shoulds*, and know that falling victim to a life of *shoulds* isn't your fault or anyone else's. Our society has pushed it onto you. And you *do* have the power to reclaim your life for you in every moment.

There are going to be a lot of layers to pull back, but I got you. We are going to uncover what's underneath every known and unknown *should* that you are living by. And now that your eyes and ears are open to all that the word carries, you can see every *should* as a speed bump, flagging your attention to slow down and question why it's there and what is beneath it.

By committing to F'ing the *shoulds*, you will be freeing and healing yourself from doubt, fear, judgment, expectation, guilt, shame, worries, and more, every single day! You will become present to what it is you are saying, thinking, believing, and the *whys* behind it all. You will gain a direct line to your intuition and develop radical compassion for yourself and your fellow humans living in this *should* world.

Day in and day out, we are wearing the heavy weight of *should* like an invisible, itchy, and inescapable cloak. It's time to take it off and start your journey of kicking out the *shoulds* for good!

CHAPTER 2

DO THE WANTS.

All of those years ago, when I was grieving the sudden death of my father, leaving my dream career of being a touring sound engineer, and discovering the internal message that I was done with *shoulds*, I chose to fully commit to eliminating the word. I didn't ease into it or try to just notice where I felt a *should*. From the start, I was 100,000 percent committed (and am still just as committed). I can vividly remember being in a conversation and starting to say, "We shou . . ." and would just be stuck there mid-*should*, looking around, searching for another word to use instead. I would catch the *should* as it was coming out of my mouth but then be stuck there thinking, *Well, what other word can I use?*

After these public pauses and stutters happened a few times, I realized that in order to fully eliminate the *shoulds*, I had to have a word at the ready to replace it with. Every time that *should* tried to stumble out of my mouth or popped up in my mind, I thought, *Well, how can I say this now? What do I say instead of* should? *What am I really trying to say or ask? This* is where the true work showed up and also where the true magic showed up. I wasn't just kicking a word out of my vocabulary. I was taking full control of my word choices, which led me to look deeply at what I was actually saying, to examine my thoughts, and to question my beliefs as I deprogrammed and empowered myself all day long. All of that simply by swapping out *should* for what I discovered was this ideal word (in most cases). That word was and remains to this day to be **want**. I didn't get to **want** right away, though. I tried out (and on) other words, but they just didn't really create that much of a shift for me.

Need was one of the first words that came up as a possible *should* replacement, and *must* popped up often too. But these two substitutes honestly didn't feel great. I mean, sure, I wasn't saying *should,* but it didn't *feel* much different.

I *should* wake up earlier.
I *need* to wake up earlier.
I *must* wake up earlier.

I *should* call my mom back.
I *need* to call my mom back.
I *must* call my mom back.

I *should* think about new job possibilities.
I *need* to think about new job possibilities.
I *must* think about new job possibilities.

Need and *must* both create a sense of urgency that could be motivating, but they still left me feeling the heavy, unfun, pushy energy of *should.* In some ways they even felt more punishing and demanding than *should.* Like if I didn't do those things *now,* then I was lazy, a failure, wrong. I wasn't looking to be meaner to myself or to order myself or anyone else around. So those words quickly got dismissed.

Could as a replacement for *should* felt a little more spacious, as it introduces the idea of possibilities. It shows that I have a choice in the matter.

I *should* do the dishes.
I *could* do the dishes.

I *should* be eating healthier.
I *could* be eating healthier.

I *should* really think about what I am
going to do next.
I *could* really think about what I am
going to do next.

But *could* also feels more like that emoji with the arms out to the sides and the palms up. Like, well, maybe . . . I don't know? I could . . . ? *Could* felt like it gave me a choice, which was moving in the right direction for me and definitely felt better in conversations. But it also didn't really motivate me to make a choice *and* get into action. *Could* works, but it still didn't feel like my ideal go-to word.

Then there is *can*, which feels like an invitation to explore and sort of like an affirmation. Like "Yes, I can!"

I *should* go to bed earlier.
I *can* go to bed earlier.

I *should* get in some exercise today.
I *can* get in some exercise today.

I *should* return all of those e-mails today.
I *can* return all of those e-mails today.

19

Honestly, *can* feels nice; it feels like, "Hmm that is something I may explore and may even be called into doing." It is affirming. Like a light, "Yep, that is an option *and* I am capable of it." Yet it still didn't feel like the word I was searching for.

And then there was **want**. Ah, **want**—it just felt and still feels so freaking good to say, to claim, to explore, to allow! It feels so direct yet expansive, and it puts the focus on me, which sometimes can actually feel uncomfortable, but is necessary. It stretches me and nudges me to be clear with myself and others. It demonstrates that there is a choice here. A choice for me to make for myself, in this moment, based on what is happening now, what I believe now, what works for me now. Which is such a relief, to be constantly checking in with the me of right now. Not the Tricia of last year, last month, last night, but *now*. It snaps me out of the weight of the *should* that has shown up and brings me straight back to me.

I should stop scrolling on my phone.
I want to stop scrolling on my phone.

What should I do today?
What do I want to do today?

I should drink more water.
I want to drink more water.

The energies of *should* and **want** are so different, as are the implications. Feeling that shift after substituting **want** for *should* is what really locked me into fully eliminating *should* from my speech and thoughts for good. Not just for the one lost summer that I was grieving the loss of my father and searching for a way to make a difference in the world, but every single day since then.

This intentional word swap forced me to be inquisitive about what I was doing and why. It nudged me to look at what mattered to me and why. I was no longer unconsciously defaulting to the *shoulds*, which had come from a place of lack, of not enough-ness, and had me looking outside of myself to compare and "keep up." Instead, I was constantly coming back to and exploring my own **wants**. Which had me expanding, imagining, believing in, and supporting myself daily.

IT'S NOT JUST A WORD EXCHANGE, IT IS AN ENERGY EXCHANGE.

Once **want** entered the playing field of choices to replace *should*, holy shit, did that change *everything*!

I would wake up and stumble out of bed with no job and no idea what I was doing with my life and would catch myself thinking, *What* should *I do today? Wait! What do I* **want** *to do today?*

The full body energetic shift from *should* to **want** was felt immediately. With *should*, my body would tighten, my shoulders would crowd in, my stomach would clench—it felt tense, stress-ridden, rushed, forced, and heavy. But with **want**, my shoulders relaxed back, my chest expanded, my breathing became deeper, and my entire body energy would transform and feel more grounded and open. I would feel myself landing back into my body.

Just by swapping this one word I could feel my body and mind expand with the realization that I had given myself a choice. That I was now looking within myself for my answer instead of searching outside of myself or looking for it within all of the *should* files I had unknowingly collected in my mind. Even when it felt uncomfortable because it was challenging me to dig deeper to be honest with myself and others to get clear on my **want**, it still felt so much better than *should*, as I was becoming more connected to myself.

All our lives, we are collecting information, opinions, advertisements, and directives. We are collecting *shoulds* without knowing it! This is how I *should* look, dress, talk, assert myself (or not), work, eat, take care of myself, act in a relationship, create a family, etc. We have been brainwashed in a way. There has been a huge machine of both fear and love working to create these *shoulds*. Don't get upset with yourself for collecting all of this *should* data and living into it. It is not your fault if you have been blindly living out something that was sold to you as a *should*. It won't help you to be hard on yourself or beat yourself up for it. Simply notice it, acknowledge it, and then realize that you get to shift it!

> You get to ask yourself, "What do I **want**?"
> And *you* get to explore that and answer it for *yourself*.

It may seem like such a small thing. But I am telling you, swapping out that one word made me so mindful of what I was actually saying, doing, believing, and feeling. And I felt the energetic swap instantly! Why, not try it?

WAIT, WHAT DO I WANT?

F'ing the *shoulds* became my new way of life. All day, every day, I was now asking myself, "What do I **want**?" Sure, a lot of it was small stuff, but our days are made up of the small stuff. And each small *should*-to-**want** swap helped me uncover *why* I was making those choices, which revealed the really deep stuff that was weighing on me, limiting me, and holding me back.

What *should* I do today?
What do I **want** to do today?

What *should* I eat for breakfast?
What do I **want** to eat for breakfast?

What *should* I wear today?
What do I **want** to wear today?

I *should* exercise.
I **want** to exercise.

Should I go to the grocery store?
Do I **want** to go to the grocery store?

I *should* be more social. I haven't been home
this much in years.
Do I **want** to be social?

Weighing out my **wants**, instead of coming to everything from the place of *should*, helped me to navigate a time in my life that was full of both clarity and uncertainty. I was so moved with purpose to create change in the lives of others, to wake them up to truly living *their* lives. But I had no fucking clue how I would do that. Not to mention that I had just quit my career with zero savings to back me up. I was incredibly lucky to be able to cat-sit and live rent-free in the home that belonged to the artist whose tour I had just left since he would be on the road all year. And I was able to get a zero-percent-interest credit card, but I knew those were both temporary placeholders.

I had been working my dream job since the age of 19. It was thrilling and fulfilling work that dominated my life. So if there was a wedding or party or anything taking place when I was on tour, there was no question that I'd have to miss it. Being a touring sound engineer wasn't a career where you could call in sick or request a vacation week, but that never really bothered me, because I loved my job and the life it gave me. But because of this, I was used to not having a choice in a lot of social matters. It was a yes if I was home and a no if I wasn't.

Having this blank space of time opened up a whole new world of considering my **wants** and being given a true choice to say yes and no. And honestly that was a little scary. I was no longer just saying yes because I *should* since I could and going with the default answers that were implanted in me and being fed to me. I was truly checking in with, What do I **want**? What does the Tricia of right now enjoy? What do I **want** to spend my time doing? And who did I **want** to do it with?

That entire summer was like attending the brand-new school of Tricia. For someone who had been on a self-love, self-care, and personal development journey since claiming my life at the age of 15 and had always felt connected to her intuition, I had no clue how much learning about myself I was about to do!

Do I **want** to go to that wedding?

Do I **want** to spend time with that friend?

Do I **want** to spend time alone?

What am I doing just because it feels like I *should*?

What am I doing just because it feels expected of me?

Taking the *shoulds* out of my life and swapping them out for **wants** opened up a space of constant evaluation within myself. All day long I was exploring what felt like a *should*, why it felt like a *should*, and where that *should* came from. It got me to look deeper at how I truly felt and why I felt that way. It helped me to get crystal clear in each moment about what was true for me and what was motivating my actions, thoughts, and mood. Were those my real thoughts, feelings, and desires, or was I being overrun by what I thought I *should* be doing, feeling, being?

By exchanging my *shoulds* for my wants, I was instantly reminded that I am here, living, breathing, existing. This is my life. Am I living it in my own honor? Or am I merely following the *shoulds* that have been taught to me and are ingrained in my mind? Each and every day, I discovered how the *shoulds* of life and the actual word *should* had been holding me back and shaping me. And so, every single day I was confronting *and* healing myself over and over and over again.

> By exchanging my *shoulds* for my **wants**, I was instantly reminded that I am here: living, breathing, existing. This is my life.

These became questions that I started to ask myself regularly as I got more and more tuned in to the *shoulds*. (P.S. I still ask myself these questions regularly.)

- Do I **want** to?
- Do I enjoy that?

- How do I feel when I am with them?
- How do I feel when I do that?
- Why do I do that? Is it a **want** or a habit, or what I think other people want or expect from me?
- Is that true for me?
- Why am I saying yes?
- Why do I feel like I *should*?

THE *SHOULD* SHIFT

Asking myself these questions and calling out every *should* that came my way in order to swap it out for **want** didn't mean that I was automatically tossing out and abandoning every single thing that surfaced as a *should*. I learned to use the word and feeling of *should* as a sign to lean in and get curious. Instead of blindly following the *shoulds*, I went on a little (or deep) excavation process to get clear on my actions, intentions, feelings, and more. A lot of times, calling out a *should* and swapping it with a **want** meant going against the *should* and kicking it out of my day/life. *But* there were a number of times that I ended up reframing what initially showed up as a *should* as a true personal **want**. And coming to something from a place of **wanting** to, instead of from a place of *should*, completely shifted how it showed up to me and how I showed up for it. I was making choices with my heart and my mind, with consideration for myself and for others.

If someone I loved spending time with invited me to do something that wasn't my top pick, I didn't jump in with an immediate yes. I allowed myself to check in with what I really felt, what I really **wanted**. I saw that yes, I **wanted** to spend time with this person, but instead of seeing a show at a loud bar like they suggested, I **wanted** to suggest meeting them for a walk or an early dinner and a glass of wine.

When friends asked me to help them (since I was unemployed and appeared to not be doing anything at all), I weighed out why I would **want** to help instead of just saying yes because I *should*. I saw I didn't have to say yes just because I could. I may not have had employment, but I was working. I was working on myself, I was grieving, I was healing. Even if others couldn't understand that and just saw me as someone with loads of time on my hands, I could still value my own personal space and time. Or I could say yes while still making space for myself each day and not allowing myself to be overrun with showing up for others just because I wasn't clocking in to a job everyday. I was taking care of me, and that was a reason on its own.

When I was faced with the "what *should* I eat today" question, I didn't go full throttle on eating all the things I had told myself I *shouldn't* eat for years because *I can eat whatever I want!* I did allow myself to eat those **wants**, *and* I explored the question, "Why do I feel I *should* eat salad instead of pizza?" Oh, right, because the salad makes me feel energized for the rest of the day and the pizza makes me feel tired and bloated. When I felt like I *should* get out of bed in the morning, instead of pushing myself out with shame for feeling lazy, I gave myself permission to either stay in bed *or* ask myself, "Why do I feel I *should* get up now? What do I **want** to do today?" And then that would motivate me to either get up and get to it *or* to luxuriate in the fact that I was allowed to start my day and spend it how I wished, so if I wanted to lounge in bed and it was supporting me, why not?

I even got offered some work opportunities during this time from past employers and co-workers who knew I had no income coming in and wanted to support me. I was able to come to each opportunity from a true **want** space instead of *I* should *take advantage of this opportunity to earn money.* I said yes to some sound work, even though I was clear that sound was no longer my path. I didn't take those jobs because I *should* take advantage of the income and be grateful that they had thought of me. I took them because I **wanted** to. In fact, I had to fight myself over feeling that I *shouldn't* take the sound jobs because I had quit sound! I got clear with myself that yes, I did quit sound as my forever career *and* I **wanted** to say yes to these nondemanding short-run gigs while I was figuring out my next steps.

At first it may feel impossible or exhilarating or both to truly eliminate all *shoulds* from your life. It may seem like by eliminating *shoulds* and choosing your own personal **wants** that you will stop doing a lot of things. You may have thought or still be thinking, *Yeah, right. I cannot live a life purely of my own* **wants***. I would turn into a selfish asshole; plus, it is just unrealistic.* Well, you won't! It's not! You will turn into the most self-aware, compassionate, empowered version of you yet, and that will only keep growing as you stay on the ~~should~~/**want** evolution.

LIVING YOUR WANTS IS NOT SELFISH

Something that I see over and over again about the word *want* and the idea of allowing ourselves to choose and live out our **wants** is the fear that it is selfish. People can feel confronted by the idea that they actually get to choose what they **want**. This idea of considering, choosing, and living by your own **wants** feels wrong to some, feels entitled to others, and may even feel impossible.

I get that. I do. But I am going to call bullshit on that and break it down for you so that you can see that being aligned, in integrity, and living your **wants** is the least selfish thing that you can do. Living your **wants** doesn't just serve you, it serves everyone whom you come in contact with and has a ripple effect that spreads out into the world at large. Yes, really. Being in alignment with your **wants** shifts your energy, and that is something that not only *you* feel, but others can feel too.

Many of us have been raised to be givers, caretakers, or people pleasers. We want to be generous, good-hearted, compassionate people. Those are all amazing things to be (well, maybe not the people pleaser, which will definitely come up in later chapters). I want you to know, and I will prove to you that you can be a generous, good-hearted, compassionate person while still living your **wants**. Actually it will likely result in you being an even more generous, good-hearted, compassionate person! And the added bonus is that you will show up in the world with an even clearer head, heart, energy, and intentions.

> You can be a generous, good-hearted person while still living your **wants**, and the bonus is that you will show up with an even clearer head, heart, energy, and intentions.

Shifting from *shoulds* to **wants** doesn't automatically mean that you only do what serves you. It means that you put more attention and intention into what you are doing and why. So that when you say yes, when you show up, when you support others, you are clear that you are doing so because you **want** to, not because you feel like you *should*, which is an *entirely* different energy.

Trust me, I know it can sound impossible to live a life purely of your own **wants**. But it is possible. By using each *should* that comes at you daily as an opportunity to dive deeper into yourself, you will expose *why* you are doing what you are doing and get clear on whether or not this is a **want** for you right now. In the following chapters, you will start to reveal to yourself what has been motivating your choices, let go of the *shoulds* that aren't for you, claim what really is a **want** for you, and what things you **want** to shift from a *should* to a **want** because you **want** the end result.

You can skip forward to Chapter 9 to look at some real-life *should*/**want** swaps that will get you to do the dishes, run the errands, have the tough conversations, and other things that you may struggle to see as **wants** but that do need to happen. Before I get there, though, I am going to expose the deeper layers of this six-letter word so that you can begin to uncover and understand what it has been doing to you all of these years.

YOU ARE WORTHY OF YOUR WANTS

Let me be clear. I know firsthand that you can't just wave a magic wand, state your **wants**, and get them. You can't always have what you **want** in this moment. But what you can do is to allow yourself to explore what it is that you **want**, crave, and dream of. Instead of shooting yourself down, you can allow yourself to explore even the smallest ways to plant seeds for your **wants** and make space for them to grow. So often we don't even allow ourselves to get a glimpse of our true **wants** because they feel impossible, out of our current reach, or we have some self-worth issue talking us out of it. Our subconscious dismisses it before we are even fully aware that it is a **want**. Not anymore. It is time to shine a light on your **wants**.

> You can't always have what you **want**—in this moment. But what you can do is to allow yourself to explore what it is you do **want**, crave, or dream of.

It also may take you some time to really get clear on your **wants**; that is okay too. Instead of feeling like you *should* know what you **want**, allow yourself the space, the safety, the peace to allow it to come. So often we are in a rush to have our answer that we end up defaulting to someone else's. Uncovering what you **want** in all the small, everyday ways and the really huge, life-changing ways—perhaps after a lifetime of never considering what *you* **want**—may bring up a lot. You don't have to rush it or run from it. Keep digging in and know that by leaning into the discomfort you will be opening up space for so much freedom, joy, fulfillment, and more. Allow yourself the space to feel it all.

You are worthy of your **wants**.

Give your **wants** a chance.

Give yourself a chance.

"Shifting from *shoulds* to wants doesn't automatically mean that you do only what serves you. It means that you put more attention and intention into what you are doing and why."

CHAPTER 3

SHOULDS ARE AT THE ROOT OF OUR DOUBTS AND FEARS.

As I said, I was *not* a person who felt that I lived a life of *shoulds*. I was living my dream life! When I wasn't touring with music icons such as Natalie Cole and Dolly Parton, I traveled on my own. I did life my way. Yet when I committed to banning *should* from my vocabulary, all my doubts, fears, and worries were exposed. Damn.

Each day we are absorbing so much information, advice, and *shoulds*. And even when our life isn't full, we find things to distract ourselves. Sometimes the search to better ourselves *is* a distraction from actually allowing ourselves to fully see and feel what it is we are thinking and believing about ourselves. We don't often give ourselves the space to look at the doubts, fears, and worries that sabotage us and talk us out of what we **want**. We don't question the thoughts that have us believing that we are lacking and keep us seeking our answers outside of ourselves.

When I chose to just focus on this one word, so much became clear to me. It was astonishing. Simply by bringing my attention to this one word, I gave myself an everyday, all-day access point to get real and face the doubts, worries, and fears that were holding me back. When recording an episode for my podcast with Dan Peres, the award-winning former editor-in-chief of *Details* and author of *As Needed for Pain,* I told him about my *should*/**want** theory and he nailed it with his assessment, "It's a really powerful concept and an incredibly powerful life hack. It slows down your process and lets you look at what is motivating your behavior."

GET CURIOUS

So often in life we are frozen in fear and self-doubt that we don't take the actions we **want** in life. We often don't even allow ourselves to think outside of our current circumstances because of our deep-rooted doubts and fears. By completely tuning in to the word *should*, you will gain access to what you are feeling and why you are feeling it, and be able to move through and shift your fears, doubts, worries, judgments, and more. Having sudden clarity on what you have been telling yourself may be uncomfortable, but that is where the growth happens. You may want to push past what comes up. Or you may try to just automatically project yourself into what you **want** to believe instead of allowing yourself to see and feel into the stories that have been holding you back. I promise you that the way to truly move through and overcome the doubts and fears that have been holding you back is to look them in the eye, get to know them, and get curious about them so

"Sometimes the search to better ourselves *is* a distraction from actually allowing ourselves to fully see and feel what it is we are thinking and believing about ourselves."

that you can see what beliefs you need to work on in order to get clear on who you are, what you want, and what *is* possible for you.

You *can* allow yourself to hear your doubts, fears, and worries and thank them for their protection while choosing to move forward without them weighing you down. Our minds are good at developing doubts, fears, judgments, and more in the form of *shoulds*, but you don't have to take them as the truth. You can redirect them and re-create them. Give yourself permission to get curious about what it is you are telling yourself!

SELF-DOUBT HOLDS US HOSTAGE IN OUR OWN LIVES

What doubts have been holding you back? One of my past clients, Tara, dreamed of being a therapist, but her goal kept getting squashed by her own doubts and her belief in what other people said. "You are too old to go to graduate school." "You aren't cut out for college." Her friends and co-workers who truly knew her told her she would make an amazing therapist. But her doubts were louder. She thought that it was too late. That she *should* have pursued it sooner. That she *should* stay where she was. She wouldn't be able to be a therapist, so why even try?

She was in college, pursuing her degree but living a double life. She had all of these dreams and desires, but her doubts kept nagging at her, saying that she *should* just give up. Once she graduated with a bachelor's degree, a new world of possibilities opened for her, but she kept holding herself back. She was working at a job she hated, and longed to live alone, to attend graduate school to become a therapist, and to be working in the field helping people. She and I worked together to uncover her doubts and fears and what was layered beneath those *shoulds* that she kept hearing.

At the time I am writing this, Tara is counseling youth who are affected by trauma, is pursuing her master's degree in psychology, and living on her own in an apartment that she loves. She is working at the most rewarding and challenging job she has ever had and is the first in her family to be in grad school, where her ideas of what a therapist *should* be are challenged every day.

Said Tara, "The narrative I told myself for so long, the doubts that held me back, I knew deep down they were not correct, but I held on to them for so long because my biggest fear was failing. I need to have all the answers; I need to work on my healing and be 'fixed' or perfect. I *should* be younger; I *should* have it all figured out. *I now know that I was failing myself by not at least trying to go after my desires.* I was doubting myself, and by doing that, I was failing to live to my full potential. What I have come to see is that I have the choice regardless of the *should*—and I chose to live the life I **want** to have."

DOUBT YOUR DOUBTS

I've always loved the phrase "doubt your doubts." I was in a yoga class at least 10 years ago when a yoga teacher said this, and it has been one of my favorite mantras ever since. I mean, take a moment with that phrase. Doesn't it feel like a huge release? Like, wait a minute, so I am not stuck with these shitty thoughts that keep clinging to my mind and are trying to drag me down? I am allowed to

"You *can* allow yourself
to hear your doubts, fears,
and worries and thank them
for their protection
while choosing to move
forward without them
weighing you down."

doubt those motherfucking doubts? It's liberating, right? The only problem is that you need to be aware that you are having a doubt in order to have the power to doubt it.

This is the magic of the full commitment to *should* elimination. You will be exposing your doubts daily as you overthrow the pesky *shoulds* and get clear on what lies beneath them. You will be guided to reclaim yourself, instead of automatically falling into *should* holes. You will be unearthing them and remodeling your personal belief system on a moment-to-moment basis as you get clear on your **wants**.

It may take some time for you to get used to naming the fears and doubts that are hidden in the *shoulds*, but the more committed you are to their elimination, the quicker your subconscious will be exposed! One way to incorporate a doubt/fear check-in every day (or when you remember to) is to ask yourself straight up:

What is a doubt I am hearing/believing/living?

What am I afraid of?

What *should* am I hearing?

What doubt is underneath it?

For example, when you think, "I *should* be more like _____," you are doubting your value and your capabilities. When you think, "I *should* be further along," you are doubting your worth, your journey, and what is possible for you. When you think, "They *should* have replied by now," you may be doubting yourself and how that person feels about you. You may be afraid they are ignoring you or that they don't even like you, when really maybe they just haven't had the space to see your message and reply or they just forgot!

Name the *shoulds*, the doubts, the fears, and then remember that you get to doubt them! Question them! Ask yourself if you really believe in them, or if you have taken on someone else's beliefs. Instead of trying to run and hide from your doubts and fears, confront them. Diving into your doubts and fears may seem scary, but just by naming them you are taking away their power.

> Name the *shoulds*, the doubts, the fears, and then remember that you get to doubt them!

Getting curious with your doubts and fears will give you the space to dream, get creative, give yourself hope, and set yourself free. You will be kicking doubts to the curb all day long as you call out *shoulds* and open yourself up to your **wants**!

SELF-DOUBT DOESN'T HAVE AN EXPIRATION DATE

We may think we have the whole believing-in-ourselves and self-love thing down. We are sure we are living true to ourselves, going after what we **want**, being who we truly are, but then the hard stuff (and even the good stuff) can send us straight back into doubts, fears, judgments, and the *shoulds* they are often hiding behind. Yep, doubts and fears are often triggered when life is good!

This happened to me when I was entering a romantic partnership, when I became a mother for the first time, and again when I put myself out there and said, "Hey, world. I am going to write a book about this life-changing thing I do."

During the early months of dating, I found myself questioning what I *should* wear, what restaurant I *should* choose, what I *should* order, when I *should* text, and on and on. I was questioning everything, and I considered myself to be a strong, independent, confident, decidedly unique individual who empowers others to *own their awesome*! And yet the butterflies of love, and the desire of wanting to be loved and accepted as I am, had me second-guessing myself in many small ways that were really hiding the big ways I was questioning myself and my worth. I was fighting the *shoulds everywhere*. Even though *should* had been long gone from my vocabulary, I felt its energy making me question myself and my worth.

I had wanted to be a mother my whole life. When I felt I had met my partner, I set up my life to become a mother. I didn't feel worried at all. And then my first daughter arrived, and I became a stressed-out mess. I read all the mom blogs, looking for answers on what I *should* do. I mean yes, researching and gathering what works for people with experience is a good thing! But when it totally overwhelms your ability to think and choose for yourself and your ability to trust yourself, it's gone too far. When I started to trust myself to know what was best for my daughter and pay attention to her cues instead of living with a running tally of *shoulds* weighing on me, I was able to relax and enjoy my own way of mothering.

When I finally got my ass in gear to write this book (my first), I was standing tall and proud. I felt connected to myself and my mission as I was writing my book proposal to sell my ideas to literary agents, hoping they would see something in me and what I had to say. And then the *shoulds* started to overwhelm me. All the comparisons to other authors, coaches, speakers—*everyone*—popped up, along with *should* advice from other authors, agents, and people who had no experience with writing a book or the publishing world. Each time I started to doubt myself, I tuned in and remembered what I **wanted**. I reminded myself of why I **wanted** to do it and let my **want** and why push me to keep trying, showing up, and making progress.

> The doubts will come, but they don't have to stick to you. Name them, question them, and dig deeper into the truth of who you are and what you are capable and worthy of.

FROZEN IN FEAR

Once upon a time, I almost sabotaged one of the biggest opportunities of my career. I was a 25-year-old woman who was working in a position that was and still is super rare for a woman to have. In order to get myself to this place in my career, after becoming a sound engineer at age 19 without knowing anything about it except that I wanted to do it for a living, I lived by this Eleanor Roosevelt quotation:

> *No one can make you feel inferior*
> *without your consent.*
>
> — ELEANOR ROOSEVELT

I was constantly subjected to people doubting that I would be good at my job just because I was young and female. But instead of letting it stop me, I reminded myself over and over that **they can't make me feel inferior unless I believe that I am.** It was my constant internal reminder and a mental adjustment for me to make when dealing with other people's projections of me. I could have let their shit-talking, assumptions, attitudes, and judgments make me doubt myself, but instead I reminded myself that I was capable, I was willing, I was learning, and I kept showing up. Later, when I actually did know what I was doing, I still got those judgments because I was still female and young—I reminded myself that I was good at my job and let my work speak for itself.

This led to me being chosen as the monitor engineer for a true living legend, Dolly Parton. I was flown across the country for the day and driven to her personal recording studio for a one-on-one meeting/hang so that she could check me out and approve of me before she okayed me as her new sound engineer. I was so honored to be chosen. I mean, *holy shit*! I was working with Dolly freaking Parton! But I was also deeply afraid of not being good enough and messing everything up, and instead of admitting that to myself, and supporting myself to work through the fears, I just kept pushing the fears deeper and deeper down.

In my entire career up to this point, I had spoken up about what I didn't know, asked for help if I didn't feel 100 percent certain, and asked lots of questions. I always felt I would rather ask questions and double-check my assumptions rather than assume I knew something and then mess it all up.

The pressure I put on myself for this tour caused me to flip the way I thought and handled myself. Because I was working for Dolly, I felt everyone expected me to be one of the best sound engineers in the world who knew absolutely everything and did not need any help. I said yes to working with equipment I had never used before because I was afraid to say no. I was too afraid to speak up when the bandleader purchased ridiculous gear that I knew wasn't right. I abandoned my intuition, my good sense, and my natural question-asking self because I was afraid of seeming like I didn't know what I was doing. It made no sense, because if I was playing the part of being the best of the best, then wouldn't I be speaking up about the things I knew wouldn't work, asking for what I wanted, and voicing my opinion?

It was a disaster. I was a disaster. I was so frozen in fear. The fear of not being good enough. The fear of being discovered as a fraud. The fear of speaking up and not being liked. The fear of messing up. Since I had been hired for this tour and approved by Dolly herself, I felt I *should* fit this impossible standard, and that meant not admitting that I needed help or asking any questions.

I was a good sound engineer. I was known for being able to manage a lot of chaos, instruments, microphone inputs, musicians (and their personalities), and what each band member wanted to hear coming through their onstage or in-ear monitors each night so they could perform at their best. This was a big tour. I really could have killed it, but I allowed my doubts and fears to take a front seat and sabotage me. I was honestly a crashing ship, on the edge of getting fired, when I got real with myself about the mess I was making.

PUT YOUR FEARS IN THE SPOTLIGHT

It wasn't comfortable or easy to face my own bullshit and to acknowledge to myself, the band, and the crew that I had been doing a shit job. But I needed to see past those fears that had me making poor choices. They had freaking hired me for a reason, and I **wanted** to turn this around. I started by asking other, more experienced sound engineers for support and advice on the equipment and setup. I admitted mistakes I had made, and I spoke up about what I saw wasn't working.

I was able to reroute and get myself on more stable ground by admitting that I didn't fully know what I was doing! Aha! What overturned my doubts and fears was admitting that my biggest fear was that other people would think I wasn't good enough and that I didn't know what I was doing. I outed myself, and—bam!—while the fears and doubts didn't magically disappear after I exposed them, they lost their power over me.

Kind of like kids and their fear of the dark. They aren't afraid of the actual dark so much as what may come out when it is dark. Use your new awareness of *shoulds* to turn a spotlight on your fears so that you can expose and move through them.

IT TAKES MORE WORK TO HAVE A FEAR THAN IT DOES TO LEAN IN TO IT

You may not think that you live a life full of fears, but they are always lurking and hiding out in your mind, influencing your beliefs about yourself and what is possible. Every day we have the opportunity to face our fears. Many fears we are aware of, but many we are not. In our daily lives we are often:

- Afraid to speak up
- Afraid that when we do speak up, we won't say the "right" thing, the "right" way
- Afraid of hurting people's feelings
- Afraid of making a change
- Afraid of not getting a return to our e-mail, call, message
- Afraid of getting a no
- Afraid to ask for help
- Afraid of being alone
- Afraid of not being able to pay our bills
- Afraid of being judged
- Afraid that what we are working toward and dreaming of will never happen
- Afraid that our dreams might actually come true
- Afraid that we are going to make the wrong choice
- Afraid that we are too late
- Afraid that we will lose someone that we love and respect
- Afraid that we aren't enough
- Afraid that people don't see the person we truly are
- Afraid that people will only think of us in a way that we don't want them to

Sounds fun, doesn't it? We carry around all of these fears, with new and old ones popping up constantly. Remember, the first step to overcoming a fear is to recognize

"We try to push our fears away, to bury them deep down. We fear that acknowledging them will make them come true, but really, when we turn the lights on them, we begin to break free from them."

it. Pay more attention to what is going on in that head of yours by tuning in to those *should* thoughts and feelings!

Are you making up a story or situation that isn't even actually happening? Are you stopping yourself because of a fear? Are you worrying because of a fear? Are you doubting because of a fear?

Something that I realized years ago is:

Having a Fear Is Actually More Work Than Stepping Into a Fear.

Living In Fear Takes More Energy Than Leaning In to That Fear.

By not taking action on a fear, it lives within you, weighing you down, running your life in the background. Sometimes it is so deep in you that you don't even see all the ways that you are holding yourself back, sabotaging yourself, and abandoning yourself. For example, for years I told myself and others that I could never live in LA with kids because of the traffic. It took me years to see that it was an excuse for the deep-rooted fear that I wasn't allowing myself to acknowledge, which was that I believed I was not someone who could afford to live in LA with kids. That belief was really a fear that kept me from even considering all the reasons that I did want to move back and all the ways that I could become someone who could afford to live in LA with kids.

By naming your fear and taking action (even if that action is just to start to explore the fear), you get a result, an answer, some direction on where to go next. Living in fear drains your battery; stepping into fears gives you more source energy.

Facing your fears gets easier with practice, which means you are going to want to start practicing ASAP. Often when you are living in fears and doubts and letting them run your life, it is because you are focusing on what you think other people (including the ones you love and look up to) will think of you instead of getting clear on what it is that *you* think and believe about *you*.

WORST-CASE SCENARIO

Years ago, I remember feeling the tug of emotions when I knew it was time to have a conversation with my partner about the future of our relationship. He was older and didn't talk much about the future. And by not much, I mean not at all. Meanwhile, I had gotten myself off the touring circuit to build a business with the intention of creating space to have kids. I told him from the start I wanted children as a way to let him out of the relationship early on, as I meant business and wasn't up for a casual romance at that time in my life. But during the length of our relationship, whenever I had brought up a future with babies, he never said much in return, which left me confused. I was at that point where I wanted a confirmed yes or no. I just wanted a clear answer from him. But I was so scared! What if he didn't want what I wanted? What if he wasn't ready? What if he never wanted kids and just thought I would change my mind and eventually move on?

I put off the conversation because I didn't want to be heartbroken. I didn't want to have to start over and look for a new partner when I loved the one I was with. I was so afraid to face these feelings and the reality that could come with the conversation. So I got real with myself and asked,

"Often when you are living in fears and doubts and letting them run your life, it is because you are focusing more on what you think other people (including the ones you love and look up to) will think of you instead of getting clear on what it is that *you* think and believe about *you*."

"Why do I **want** to have this uncomfortable conversation?"

"Why would it be in both of our best interests to do so?"

"What is the worst-case scenario of having this conversation?"

By looking deeper, I saw clearly that if my biggest fear came true, if he wasn't on the same page as me and did not want to have a family, as much as that would hurt, it would be better to have the information now. Even though it would be painful, and suck to have to start over, we could then go our own ways and do what was best for our futures. I realized that I did **want** to have this very confrontational, uncomfortable, scary-as-hell conversation, and we did. Walking myself through the *should*s to get clear on my **wants** made me super clear and grounded when we spoke. Five months later, we were pregnant with our first daughter.

WHAT DECISION ARE YOU MAKING OR NOT MAKING OUT OF FEAR?

Are you staying in a relationship because you fear you won't find someone else to love you? Are you staying in friendships that weigh you down because you fear making changes or being lonely? Are you staying in a work environment that you know is not what's best for you because you are afraid you won't be able to find anything else or are just afraid to even put yourself out there to try for something else? Are you *not* having a conversation for fear that it won't go the way that you want it to?

I am not saying your fears are not valid. They may be rooted in some truth; they may think they are protecting you. But how does it feel to live in that fear? When you stay in that fear, even if you are pushing it away so that you don't think you are really feeling it, you are limiting your full potential, your life, and your experience of joy, bliss, and purpose. You may even make daily efforts to be grateful for what you have, to see the good, and to spread positivity in your daily life. Yet your fear is living in your body, raising your stress levels, and making you unable to fully experience the joy you are worthy of claiming.

I invite you to have the audacity to question your doubts and your fears. You do have the power within you to do so.

CHAPTER 4

SEEING AND HEALING THE RESENTMENT, DISAPPOINTMENT, GUILT, AND SHAME THAT *SHOULDS* BREED.

One of my favorite quotes is from Sri Ravi Shankar: "Expectations suck the joy out of life." And that is really the freaking truth! We are constantly creating and living into expectations, often without realizing it, which leads us to being disappointed over and over again. And guess how expectations are created? From our good friend *should*! Nearly every day we are carrying around guilt, resentment, and shame because of the *shoulds* that are projected onto us from the outside world and from within ourselves.

I would like to state that expectations are responsible for 95 percent (a large, random number estimated without any research, but I mean, really) of our miscommunications and therefore our feelings of disappointment. We are constantly setting up ourselves, others, and life itself to fail us by creating expectations. We get upset because other people don't act like we think they *should* (in a way different from us). We get upset because life doesn't go the way we think it *should*. We get upset because people *should* be able to read our minds and know what we **want**. We have all of these *should* expectations, and because of this we bear the heavy weight of shame, blame, guilt, and resentment. Ugh. *Shoulds* are constantly stealing joy from us. We have to do the work to steal it back.

~~EXPECTATIONS~~ *SHOULDS* SUCK THE JOY OUT OF LIFE

Years ago, when I was dating the father of my children, we lived in different cities (about 90 minutes away) and would take turns driving to see the other person for the weekend. We had created what I thought was a routine: that when I reached his house or he reached mine, we would start our time together by going out to dinner. This was never discussed or set in stone; it is just what had always happened, and so I created the expectation that this is what we did.

One weekend, I was heading out to visit him slightly later than usual. Since I expected that we would go out to dinner together when I arrived, I drove hungry, dreaming about dinner possibilities for us. When I walked in the door to his home and saw him sitting on his couch eating a giant burrito, *I was pissed*!

WTF! Why didn't he wait for me to eat? Why didn't he tell me that he was getting something? I could have stopped on the way in. I could have eaten at home before

I left. I was seriously so upset. And while yes, his communication skills may have been lacking and he could have checked in with me, he hadn't. My first reaction was to fully put the blame on him. I was disappointed, annoyed, and angry. I don't know about you, but I do not enjoy feeling that way. So, while trying to get a hold of myself, I asked myself,

Had I created an expectation?
Where can I take responsibility?

What happened was I had created an expectation—a *should*, really—based on past experiences. I felt he *should* have waited for me to eat. He *should* have texted or called to tell me he was going to eat. I am a great communicator, so I would have texted to tell him; he *should* have done what I would have done! Oh, but if I am such a great communicator, why didn't I communicate to him that I was excited to get dinner when I arrived? Why didn't I check in to make sure we were both on the same page about having dinner together? Right. . . Okay, I see where I can take some responsibility here. He hadn't communicated with me that he was getting food before I got there, *but* I also hadn't communicated that I wanted us to get dinner together when I arrived and to make sure he was waiting for me.

WHERE CAN I TAKE RESPONSIBILITY?

Taking responsibility doesn't mean that you are saying it is all your fault and that you bear the weight of the blame; it isn't even saying that anyone's at fault. By asking ourselves, "Where can I take responsibility?" we actually allow ourselves to reclaim power in the situation, neutralize our feelings, and stop sitting in blame and resentment. In claiming some responsibility, I curbed the majority of the anger, frustration, and disappointment that I was feeling, and it showed me how I can be even clearer in the now and in the future. I could say both "I am disappointed that you ate without me" *and* "In the future, I will be clearer with what I **want** instead of setting expectations and not communicating them."

> By asking ourselves, "Where can I take responsibility?" we actually allow ourselves to reclaim power in the situation, neutralize our feelings, and stop sitting in blame and resentment.

This also shifted my attention back to the present, where I was able to then be excited that I could go get whatever I wanted to eat for dinner without needing to give an ounce of consideration to whether he would like my dining choice or not. So hey, triple win. I got clear on some expectations I had created, we had some clear communication, *and* I got my meal of choice without considering his opinions and tastes. *Woo-hoo!*

Expectations happen to the best of us, sometimes daily. And just like the *shoulds*, you don't have to feel like you failed if you find yourself disappointed by one. The easiest way to shift out of the disappointments is to:

1. Name the expectation you had created.
2. Name what you are feeling (disappointed, annoyed, ashamed).
3. Ask yourself, "Where can I take responsibility?"

You can also ask yourself, "Now that I see this and feel this, how do I want to avoid this disappointment in the future?" For example, in that situation I saw that in the future instead of assuming that he would think and act like I do, that it was best to check in with him to make sure we were on the same page. It is okay to feel what you feel. It is okay to feel disappointed. The point isn't to *should* yourself out of your feelings but to move through them. You will experience disappointment in life, but instead of living in the disappointment, what are you going to do about it?

IMPORTANT NOTE: This way of taking responsibility will not fit all situations in life. I do not want you to victim shame or blame yourself! For example, if you have been abused in any way and you had the expectation that the other person would act like a decent human being, I am not asking you to take responsibility for what happened to you or blame yourself for what happened. Also, let's say you got fired and it feels unfair. It is possible to see where you can take responsibility and see that it really isn't the work that lights you on fire, or you hadn't been pulling your weight. But it could also be that your company is downsizing and the loss of your job has nothing do with you, or that your boss fired you to hire his best friend's daughter. **Looking for ways to take responsibility will not work in all cases of disappointment.** Sometimes shitty stuff just happens in life, and you don't have to try to figure out the reason for it, and you don't even have to find the lesson in it. Sometimes it just sucks, and I don't want you to make it suck more by shaming and blaming yourself. (For these cases, I recommend reading Chapter 14.)

"Sometimes shitty stuff just happens in life, and you don't have to try to figure out the reason for it, and you don't even have to find the lesson in it. Sometimes it just sucks, and I don't want you to make it suck more by shaming and blaming yourself."

WELCOME TO THE WORLD OF POSSIBILITIES

Like I said, expectations often happen unconsciously, as do *shoulds*, but that doesn't mean that we have to surrender to always and only being an expectation creator. Just by being aware of our expectation-creating minds, we can put a pause on our expectations and be open to possibilities. *Ah*, breathe in the air of possibilities. Doesn't it just feel nicer? More expansive, more alive, more powerful?

My failed dinner plan example of creating an expectation is something we commonly do, but we also create and live into expectations in many other ways. I often stop myself from reaching out to people that I look up to and am inspired by. I can feel I want to acknowledge them, and I may even try to invite them on my podcast, but before I hit the E-mail or Message button, I pull back. The expectation that they will say no—or, even more likely, that they won't reply at all—stops me. It squashes me, really. And then I take a deep breath and switch from expectations to possibilities.

I say, "Okay, yes, those are two real possibilities. Getting a no and getting no answer. What are some other possibilities? They actually say yes! Or they reply with a thank you and that they don't have the space now, but I've created a new relationship with them that buds and grows." And so many times that is what happens! I mean, I do also get passes, no replies, or even people who say yes but then never follow up to schedule a time. But I would never get one yes if I didn't ask and break out of the expectations that try to squash and stop me.

When you find yourself with expectations, ask yourself, "What possibilities can I create?"

When you find yourself already creating results based on what you think will happen, nudge yourself out of it to allow yourself to dream up some possibilities. When you discover that you feel that you have failed because you haven't lived up to the *should* expectations you had created for yourself in the past, allow yourself to recenter and refocus. Instead of feeling shame for not reaching all of those expectations, allow yourself to look deeper at the possibilities for your life in the present. Not just the expectations you had and have, but what it is that you currently **want**. And yes, those things you expected and feel you *should* have or *should* have done may be things that you do **want**. Like you imagined by *x* age your career, income, or relationship status would be a certain way that it is not. I get that, but feeling shame is not going to magically change your circumstances and it probably won't really motivate you either; it will only make you less present to what you have accomplished and do **want**. Allow yourself to live from your present and to create possibilities for your future. You are never too late. You are never too early. You are right on time, and your possibilities are limitless once you allow yourself to see that.

MAKING A REQUEST

One thing that has really served me when I find myself in the *shoulds* of expectation—and wanting other people to show up in a way they are not—is seeing that **I have the ability to make a request**. This is something that I learned from Matthew and Terces Engelhart, workshop leaders, authors, and creators of Café Gratitude (I also learned about taking responsibility and the idea of possibilities

"You are never too late. You are never too early. You are right on time, and your possibilities are limitless once you allow yourself to see that."

from them). Terces says, "Expectations are often requests that we are afraid to make." *Oh*, I feel that. Why are we afraid to make them? Because we are afraid to speak up, afraid we will get a no; we are afraid they will change their minds about us; we are afraid to receive. We are afraid to ask for what we **want**, yet we think they *should* know/do/ be the way we expect them to be, and then we feel resentful because they aren't. I am laughing and shaking my head at this ridiculous truth, and I hope you are too.

Let's say that you are feeling resentful because you do the bulk of the housework and/or childcare duties in your home. That doesn't feel great, right? And while *yes*, you wish your roommate, partner, co-parent would just magically get their shit together and come to you saying, "You know what? I haven't been pulling my fair share of the work at home; that is all going to change now," we both know that isn't going to happen. So you have a choice: keep going with the way things are and live in resentment, keep going with the way things are and make peace with it, *or* make a request!

Even a small request is a request. Think about what it is that you do **want** and maybe go all in and make the full request—or create and offer some variations and possibilities. It may be true that the other person has a heavier workload and other responsibilities, and this is why you haven't spoken up in the past. But, hey, get creative and think of possibilities. **We can't always have what we want in the moment, but we can allow ourselves to get clear on our wants so that we can give ourselves even the smallest possibility of getting them.** This could be asking for even one hour of support on a day that your partner doesn't work. Giving them one delegated cleaning or household responsibility around the house, even a small one like being in charge of the toilet paper being stocked, is something. You can suggest and explore the possibility of chipping in with your roommates for a housecleaner once a month. And if they truly don't have the time or funds to contribute, you can get inventive, for example, by looking for a fellow mom to swap watching the kids once a week.

Maybe you feel resentful of your partner's family or work because they devote so much time to it. Make a request for a solo date night, once a week, where devices are put aside and you don't talk about work or family. Actually say, "I have a request: How about we make Friday night our time, and we put our phones and other distractions away? What do you think?" Using the term *request* may help you actually speak up and may also help them receive it, as you aren't demanding or *shoulding*; you are requesting. Allow yourself to actually have wants, to have possibilities and explore them instead of living into resentment and *should* expectations.

NAME IT

So often we are left feeling that things *should* be different, and maybe that is true, but instead of living into those shitty feelings of *should* and *should* not, you can explore them and show up to shift them for yourself!

I am someone who, even while kicking ass at life, getting shit done, and making magic happen, still often forgets about things like buying gifts and sending cards to friends and family for special occasions. When my kids started preschool, I was shocked that so many parents in the two-year-old preschool class brought in a full pizza, cupcakes, and custom gift bags for every kid in class for a birthday party. I mean, I love people and celebrating them (especially my own kids), but in the past I have not prioritized these types of things, and then—bam!—the day comes, or I see what other people have done and I question myself, feeling like, *Crap, I should have done this already! I should be prepared! I should have spent more time on this! I should be like the other parents or like my friend Arika, who always sends cards, flowers, and has every detail perfectly planned.*

I start to feel like I am not a good mom because I didn't plan a pizza party for the whole preschool. I start to feel like I am not a thoughtful, loving friend because I didn't send flowers. And the truth is, when these things happen, a part of me does wish I had prepared more, that I had put more thought, time, and attention into these types of things. So examining those *shoulds* has me facing those feelings and asking myself, "What do I **want** to do about it?"

To just see, wait a minute here . . .

What am I feeling?

I feel shame and like I am not the best mom for not being more prepared and doing more.

I feel like I am not a good friend to her because I didn't send her anything.

Why am I feeling this?—Is it rooted in a *should*? A *should* be? A *should* have?

I feel this because I feel like I *should* have gone all out like other preschool parents did.

I feel this because I saw on social media that my friend received gifts from other friends, and that makes me feel like I *should* have sent something too.

Is that the truth?

No, I am an amazing mom, and we had the best time celebrating my daughter's birthday at home, and she didn't know the difference.

No, I am a very thoughtful person who is always showering my friends with love and support. My friends feel my love. My friend status is not reliant on my gift giving.

Getting back to the truth is really healing to me. It is easy to absorb guilt and shame, but what is the truth underneath those feelings? Sometimes you need to make peace with yourself and your way of being and doing. Maybe you, like me, tend to do things last minute, *but* you still pull it off! Applaud yourself for doing it instead of feeling bad or comparing yourself to those who are early planners and doers. You get to choose to make peace with who and how you are *or* to work on that. Whatever you are beating yourself up for may just not be your strong suit or a top priority to you. Or perhaps it is a priority to you, but you currently do not have the budget, time, and space to do the things that you see peers, friends, and family members doing. That doesn't have to mean that you are not an awesome parent, friend, or family member.

Sometimes when asking myself the questions and assessing my feelings, I can still feel a little lacking or wish I had prepared better or done things differently. That's totally okay. I mean, that is how we grow, learn, and evolve—by being honest with ourselves and seeing we do **want** to do things better or different moving forward. When that happens (like when I was annoyed with myself for always buying birthday gifts at the last minute for the parties my kids got invited to), I ask myself:

What do I want to do in the future?

I really don't like rushing around on the day of the party to have a present for my kid to show up with. I **want** to be more prepared and buy gifts that I actually **want** to give and not just whatever I can find.

How can I support myself to make this want actionable?

I can buy books I like and other gifts in multiple to have on hand when occasions come up.

I can put notifications in my calendar that give me plenty of time to buy the gifts ahead of time.

Life is learning. Instead of *shoulding* on yourself, get clear on what you **want** to change about yourself and how you **want** to show up moving forward.

CLAIM IT

One major place that I have felt shame in my life is over my body. I know I am not the only one who looked up to impossibly lean, imperfection-free supermodels growing up. It didn't help having a mother who was constantly dieting. I inherited my body shame from my mother, capitalism, marketing, and the media. I remember being a kid and having my sister tease me and call me fat. I don't remember much of my childhood, but I remember that. It took me decades to work through the shame that started back then. How many of us have carried around shame because we are sold the lie that we *should* look a certain way?

So many of us feel shitty about ourselves on a daily basis because we have allowed the voices outside of us to determine how the voice inside of us feels. I mean, imagine if you grew up in a world where all sizes, colors, skin types, abilities, and orientations were celebrated, admired, and on display? Would I love to have a super fit body? Absolutely. Do I also want to enjoy my life, not spend hours every day working out and with a super limiting diet? *Yes.* Also, do I really, truly believe that someone in a leaner body has more value than someone in a larger body? F no!

So, when the body shame BS pops up for me—when I feel bloated, or have gained weight, or I try on a dress that I really want to wear and I don't feel great in—I again get to tap into that feeling and come back home to me by asking myself some questions.

What am I feeling?

Why am I feeling it? (It's okay if you don't know.)

How do I want to feel?

What can I do to support myself in feeling that right now?

I am feeling like I am not enough because of how my body feels and looks in this.

I am feeling this because I am not comfortable with my appearance.

I **want** to feel at peace with my body.

I can take a few grounding breaths while repeating a mantra and put on comfortable clothes that I feel good wearing.

"So many of us feel shitty about ourselves on a daily basis because we have allowed the voices outside of us to determine how the voice inside of us feels."

The truth is, it doesn't feel good when clothes don't look or feel great on my body. Yet I don't have to let that ruin how I feel about myself, my worth, my place on this Earth, and the beauty, strength, and power of my body no matter what size it is. I can claim my worth right now. You can claim whatever it is you are chasing, right now. Claim your worth. Claim your success. Claim your fulfillment. In the now.

OVERCOMING GUILT

I have always dreamed of being a mom, and when I was expecting my first child, I set up my life to be able to put my full attention on her. I had no questions, no doubts about it: I planned to breastfeed her solely until she was old enough for solid foods. I truly didn't judge any parents who chose formula for their kids. I knew plenty of moms who did not enjoy breastfeeding, had no interest in it, were not able to, or it just became too challenging to juggle along with everything else in their lives. So, while I was always all for fed being best, in my mind it would only be breast for my babies.

But I wasn't making enough milk. I had consults with lactation specialists, read all the blogs, and did all the things everyone told me to do. The doctor suggested that I supplement with formula, but everything and everyone else said supplementing would mess up my milk supply more. You simply had to train your body to make more milk by pumping and feeding around the clock was the information I was given over and over again. I had either a pump or a mouth attached to my boob at all times.

At yet another doctor's appointment in which I was told she hadn't gained enough weight—we had daily visits for weight checks at that point—I finally gave in and said yes to giving my daughter some formula. She sucked it down with a loud burp and immediately passed out into the deepest nap she had taken in her young life. I felt so relieved to see her fulfilled and sleeping peacefully. And then the guilt and shame set in. Had I been starving my daughter because I was so committed to what I thought my motherhood path *should* look like? I felt guilt that I had failed by not producing enough milk.

We ended up supplementing for only a month or so as my milk supply picked up. But even during that short time I remember fighting shame when I would pull out a bottle in public to feed her. It was so fucked up that I would feel any shame for this thing I seriously never judged any other parent for doing and that was helping my daughter live and grow! I felt shame for making sure my daughter was fed! WTF! Even though I knew what I was doing was for our best, I still had some attachment to the expectation I had created for myself and what I had imagined my motherhood journey *should* be like.

Every time I felt the shame arise, I reminded myself, "I am a nurturing, loving mother right now by giving my child more calories and nutrients than my body is currently able to make. *Yes*, I am." When I felt the pangs of how it *should* be different, I would come back to accepting that yes, this wasn't what I had visualized for myself, but it was in line with becoming the nurturing, loving mother I had dreamed of. You can choose the thoughts you **want** to have—but first you may have to tell the shitty ones to F off.

"You can choose the thoughts you *want* to have— but first you may have to tell the shitty ones to F off."

RELEASING RESENTMENT

Years ago, when I was early in my career as a sound engineer working at the House of Blues in Chicago, I was lucky to be plucked by one of the top touring sound companies in the world. Most new engineers went out on tour first as a technician or assistant to the engineer in order to learn the ropes and to just be able to get out on a tour. I was lucky to skip that step and go out on my very first tour as the monitor engineer for the Grammy Award–winning singer-songwriter Mary Chapin Carpenter.

I flew off to do my first rehearsals with her and her band in NYC, prepping for the *Today* show and *David Letterman* to be my first shows with them ever (yes, I was shitting myself). I had entered the big time as a 23-year-old, and I freaking nailed it. Chapin and the band loved me and loaded me up with compliments. After a few weeks on tour with them, I was back at my Southern California sound company's headquarters enquiring about a raise. I felt that since I was making this band happier than their last engineer, then I *should* be getting the same pay he got. Who cares if he had about 20 years of experience on me and had previously worked for Fleetwood Mac and Madonna? Yes, it was my first tour ever, but I was doing the same job, with better results. Show me the money!

The owner of the sound company did not feel the same way, but he did admire me for coming forward, stating my case, and standing up for myself. I was the first female touring sound engineer they had ever hired, and I was making it clear that I didn't feel that my sex or my age had anything to do with my value. While he didn't bring up my salary to meet the ex-Madonna engineer, he took my words into consideration. We had an open talk, and for the many years that I worked for him, I felt respected and appreciated by him, and I still do to this day.

If I hadn't faced my feelings of resentment, and my feelings of what I thought I *should* be getting, I likely would have continued to feel like I was being taken advantage of and being treated and paid unfairly. So, while being upfront with my thoughts and feelings did not end up with the result that I wanted of getting a raise, it did dissolve the energy that I felt. It was like sticking a needle into a balloon and watching the air release. By bringing awareness to this resentment and facing those feelings by having a conversation, I was able to feel a change. If I had felt disrespected in that meeting, perhaps it would have led me to leaving the tour or the company, but it didn't. I got clear about the resentment, and we met each other with respect and discussed possibilities for growth in the future.

The reality was that I was on that tour because, at my starting sound engineer rate, I fit the budget the tour had, and so even if he wanted to give me the raise, it wasn't in that tour account's budget to give me one. And yes, you may be reading this and thinking, *Well yeah, of course, Tricia—it was your first tour!* I am not saying that what I felt was completely reasonable. How we feel isn't always 100 percent reasonable, and that is why clueing in to and examining all the layered *shoulds* is so key. It has us digging into and exposing thoughts and feelings that may not even make sense but are real to us. By questioning the *shoulds*, the thoughts, the beliefs, and feelings connected to them, we can come into our lives with so much more clarity, heart, and compassion for ourselves and others.

> How we feel isn't always 100 percent reasonable, and that is why clueing in to and examining all the layered *shoulds* is so key.

Most of our feelings of resentment stem from feeling like things *should* be different. Life isn't always fair, so yes, a lot of times things *should* be different! But, unfortunately we don't have magic wands to change everything that is unfair.

You don't have to live in shame, guilt, resentment, and blame. Yes, it may take some time to heal and shift. You can expect that, or rather see that as one possibility for yourself. And again, it doesn't help to pile emotions on top of emotions, so getting mad at yourself because you fell into a shame trap, or you feel like you *should* be over it by now, isn't going to help. Handle yourself with love, care, compassion—while being real with yourself so that you can heal.

CHAPTER 5

STOP BEATING YOURSELF UP FOR WHAT ALREADY HAPPENED— THE SHOULD HAVES.

We are so freaking hard on ourselves! I mean, consider how often you ruminate and berate yourself for what you think you *should* have done. I *should've* gotten more done today. I *shouldn't* have said that. I *shouldn't* have eaten that. I *should have* trusted my gut. I *should have* spoken up. I *should have* known. And on and on. We know that we cannot change the past, yet we are often letting what has already happened put a damper on our present.

Our past choices big and small can haunt us. Everything from life choices we made 10 years ago to text messages we sent 10 seconds ago. While yes, we all have things in our lives that we look back on and wish we hadn't done, hadn't said, or had handled differently, reliving our "wrongs" and beating ourselves up for them doesn't create space for healing, forgiveness, and making change from a more secure and safe place in the present.

*Should have*s are a huge way that we "*should* all over ourselves," which then leads us to fall into the shame, guilt, and resentment that I got into in the previous chapter. And while you may not be able to stop the *should haves* from entering your mind, you can change how you relate to them. My hope for you is that you allow your mind to hit Pause, remind yourself that it already happened, release any shame/guilt/resentment that comes with the *should have* thought or memory, and then allow yourself to refocus. Instead of vilifying yourself, give yourself love, compassion, and clarity so that you can create space to heal and forgive in the **now** and set yourself up to make more aligned choices in the future.

While it is unfortunately natural for us to beat ourselves up, get down on ourselves, and feel like we fucked up when we are in a *should have*, think about what a *should have* really is. It is you **wanting** better for yourself or to better yourself. It is you learning from an experience, collecting data, looking at your feelings, and **wanting** more or different from yourself. It isn't bad or wrong to **want** to see where you can evolve, grow, change, and **want** that for yourself.

> Think about what a *should have* really is. It is you **wanting** better for yourself or to better yourself. It is you learning from an experience, collecting data, looking at your feelings, and **wanting** more or different from yourself.

But instead of patting ourselves on the back for recognizing opportunities for growth, instead of extending compassion for ourselves and our previous self (even the 10-second prior self that angrily replied to a text message instead of taking some time to reply calmly), instead of facing ourselves with understanding, we shit all over ourselves and pile shitty feelings on top of shitty feelings. Or we try to dismiss what we said or did, without actually addressing the feelings that come up when we remember that *should have*, and we live with this simmering shame and guilt that doesn't allow us to fully be present, be proud of ourselves, or trust ourselves.

When another client, Zach, came to work with me, he had just gone through a breakup. As he started to recalibrate his life and priorities, he would find himself seeing how he *should have* acted differently in the relationship. How he *should have* made these shifts and changes earlier. He had been building his own startup and neglecting most other things in his life for the past 18 months, and that was part (not all) of what led to his split with his partner. They were both taking time to work on themselves and were in communication, keeping the possibility open that they might come back together after they worked on their own stuff. He could see how their breakup had triggered this space of exploration and created a big life reset in both of them but would still get caught up in these hindsight *should haves*. I told him, and I am telling you: if you have caught yourself in a *should have*, you are already proving to yourself that you have learned, grown, and evolved by seeing how you would handle it differently in this moment.

"If you have caught yourself in a *should have*, you are already proving to yourself that you have learned, grown, and evolved by seeing how you would handle it differently in this moment."

The person he was then didn't make those choices, but the person he is now would. Acknowledge that growth and show yourself more love and compassion. When you are facing your *should haves*, meet yourself with forgiveness as you get clear on the person that you **want** to be and are becoming. Instead of punishing yourself, celebrate yourself for seeing the different actions you would make now. Seriously, go ahead and give yourself a pat on the back or a high five when you catch yourself in a *should have* instead of beating yourself up for what already happened.

WHAT ALREADY HAPPENED, ALREADY HAPPENED

I don't like for people to be mad at me. I don't think that is unusual. But it is especially hard to handle when it is someone that I care about and they are mad because we don't see eye to eye on something. One day, I got an upsetting e-mail from someone with whom I had a decade-long friendship. I immediately felt attacked and hurt. The e-mail took me by surprise, especially as they were bringing up things that happened at the start of our relationship that they had never mentioned before. I reread the e-mail and gave myself some time to calm down before replying. I apparently didn't wait long enough to reply, though, as almost immediately after I hit Send, I thought:

I *shouldn't* have said that.

I *should have* said *xyz* . . .

I *should have* waited longer to reply to that e-mail.

So then I wrote another e-mail. And then another. And then another. My replies swerved from *I am so sorry; I had no idea*, to anger, to *What the actual fuck are you even talking about?*, to trying to find common ground and create space to have a conversation where we could both feel heard, seen, and have the possibility of understanding each other.

Surprisingly sending four e-mails did not make me feel any better. I really wished that what I had sent as e-mail-reply number four had been the first and only reply that I had sent, requesting that we get on the phone to talk about it. I *should have*, but I didn't.

When I am stuck in a *should have* feedback loop, simply repeating phrases like these below snap me out of beating myself up and reliving what has already been said and done to bring me back to the present moment:

- I *should have*, but I didn't.
- I wrote what I wrote.
- I said what I said.
- I did what I did.
- What already happened, already happened.
- I am here now.

Reminding myself of these simple truths allows me to slow down, calm myself, and ground myself. It helps to soothe my anxiety, frustration, anger, and more. Sometimes repeating these types of phrases is all that I need to release, relax, and keep moving forward. And sometimes this gets me out of the feedback loop, *but* it's not enough for me to be able to fully move through it and release the *should have* that is weighing on me. This was one of those cases, so I asked myself, "What can I do right now to move through these heavy feelings that won't let me focus on anything else?"

WHAT CAN I DO RIGHT NOW?

By acknowledging the *should have* and how you feel, you give yourself space to recalibrate. Instead of shoving the feelings away or sitting in that past pain and shame, give yourself a chance to see what you can do in the now, because that is where we are: the now, not the past. When you can't get out of those feelings, ask yourself: "What can I do to move through this?"

Simply remind yourself that, at the time, you did your best, even if you can now see how irrational you acted, how immature you were, how uneducated and unprepared you were. Acknowledging that you did your best—even if it is nowhere near where you think your best *should have* been, comes from the space of hindsight.

In some *should have* cases, the "What can I do to move through this?" could be checking in with the person it involves. If you feel awkward about what you said or how you said it, can you express that? Can you make amends with yourself and/or with the other person/people? Even if you are wincing from something that happened years ago and think the other people won't even remember it, approaching them may help you heal and move through it.

In some cases, it could be doing something nurturing for yourself because the *should have* isn't something you have the control to change. It could be talking to someone who is a great listener so that you have the experience of being heard, seen, and supported. It could be talking to a professional. It could be making a commitment to yourself or someone else based on what you wish you could change that already happened.

What can you do right now to support yourself, forgive yourself, ground yourself?

TAKE IT TO THE PAGE

You know how *everyone* tells you how transformative it is to journal? How it helps you to sort out your thoughts and feelings and give yourself space for your dreams, goals, and more? It really does! I personally could never get myself into journaling until I read about what Julia Cameron calls "morning pages" in her book *The Artist's Way.* Learning about this freestyle way of journaling (which I will share more about in Chapter 16) freed me up to not be so perfect and precious about it and to actually start to utilize this healing practice in my own way.

When I am struggling to work through something and can feel the heaviness weighing on me, it always works magic for me to vent it out on the page. I name what I am feeling and let my rage, pain, and frustrations all flow out of me. I channel compassion for myself and the other people involved too—even if I feel they are in the "wrong"—as I remind myself that I don't know their full story and their pain. I even put myself in the place of my past self, back to that *should have* moment, and write out and explore what actions I would take now in hindsight, if I were in that same position. This helps me to heal and forgive by doing it in a compassionate, explorative way. I may also write phrases over and over, like the ones I named on page 80, such as: "What already happened, already happened."

"By acknowledging the *should have* and how you feel, you give yourself space to recalibrate. Instead of shoving the feelings away or sitting in that past pain and shame, give yourself a chance to see what you can do in the now, because that is where we are: the now, not the past."

And I ask myself things like: "What do I want to learn from this and take with me in the future?"

In this instance, what I learned or remembered is that I prefer to talk things out in real time on a call or face-to-face, allowing space for each person to be heard and to be aware of tone and emotion instead of spending hours debating the perfect word choice and punctuation and tone that will not offend but will also get my point across clearly. E-mails and other messaging can be read from different energies and perspectives, which often makes what already hurts feel messier. This *should have* got me clear that, in the future, when I get a message that riles me up, I will reply only with a message of something like, "I would love to talk about this in real time so that I can fully hear you out and have the space to reply as well. When is good for you?"

Envisioning this future possibility released a lot of tension in my body. Even though the issue at hand had yet to be resolved or cleared up with the other person and I wasn't even sure if that would happen, I felt good about how I was setting up future Tricia, and that was calming to present Tricia and healing to past Tricia.

As for the current situation: I had already sent the e-mails. I had already requested that we talk on the phone. A lot was out of my hands. I also had to remind myself that people won't always agree with me or see things my way. No matter how right I may feel that I am. No matter how many other people agree with me. No matter how I see the facts. Everyone has their own life journeys, their own wounds, their own perspectives that are formed from their past experiences, and that is the lens through which they see, feel, and operate. It isn't always about you (even if it was triggered by you), and that doesn't mean that either of you are wrong or right.

> ### Journaling Prompts to Help You Vent It Out
> - Name what you are feeling and let the rage, pain, and frustrations all flow out of you.
> - Channel compassion for yourself and the other people involved too.
> - Put yourself in the place of your past self, back to that *should have* moment, and write out and explore what actions you would take now in hindsight.
> - Write out phrases like "What already happened, already happened."
> - Ask yourself: "What do I want to learn from this and take with me in the future?"

SOMETIMES YOU JUST DON'T KNOW— UNTIL YOU KNOW

This is another phrase that pulls me out of beating myself up and into the present moment. It is so freaking simple, yet so true. It is the reality of life. We don't know until we know. That is how life works. We are always learning, growing, evolving, and that can often mean that we step in piles of shit and miss turns along the way.

When I first started sharing notes of inspiration on the Internet, I sometimes fell into what could now be labeled as toxic positivity. I shared quotations of others and created my own affirmations that were empowering, but I can now see they could also be somewhat victim blaming and come from privileged thinking. Things like, "I create my own experience of life. Whatever experience I am having, I am creating it; therefore, I can change it." That is one of the affirmations in my first affirmation deck called *Own Your Awesome*. When I wrote it, I had learned from some mentors of mine how we can create our own experiences of life with our thoughts, beliefs, actions, and attitudes, and that empowered me. The idea was that I could shift my mindset, attitude, and approach at any moment. Looking at life this way can be very freeing and empowering, as it has you taking life into your own hands. Yet later, I began to cringe when I would see that affirmation in my deck.

When I started to wake up to the privileges I had as a white, straight, cisgender, middle class female without disabilities and looked at that affirmation in the hands of someone who was living in a world of unfair social justice, discrimination, and prejudice, it landed differently. Like, was it saying that when one of my dearest friends was treated differently in an LA juice shop because of the color of her skin, it was just a manipulation of her own mind, and she could just magically change how the world treated her—since she creates her experiences?

Or if I put myself in the position of someone suffering from mental, physical, or sexual abuse, was this something that would actually empower them to try to get out of that situation, or would they think that they had made the abuse happen, since they create their experiences of life? Would they read it and think they had they created the abuse?

I do believe that we can all use the power of our thoughts to get through challenging, unfair times and motivate ourselves to make changes in our own lives and in the world. *And* I know that there are a lot of shitty, unfair things that happen in society and our lives. This affirmation may still empower people in unfair situations to shed their inner judgments and the limitations society has set for them. But I truly don't want anyone to read that affirmation and for it to make them get down on themselves because "they have created their experiences."

I started to get upset with myself that I had put these types of affirmations out in the world, like I *should have* known better. I *should have* given those affirmations more thought and considered how they may land for people in different situations, bodies, existences. And then I reminded myself:

Sometimes you just don't know—until you know.

And parts of me still feel like, "Come on, Tricia, you had to have known, or you *should have* realized this earlier. You *should have* never even put these somewhat harmful affirmations in your card deck." But it already happened. I did put them in the deck. This affirmation is in thousands of homes around the world. And I didn't wake up until I did.

So, instead of staying in punishing-myself mode every time that I see those affirmations, I remind myself that I didn't know then, but I know now, and then ask myself,

What can I do right now?
What can I commit to moving forward?

I move myself from punishing my past self to aligning with my future self. I can commit to being more considerate of the affirmations that I share moving forward. I can edit those cards out of the deck the next time it goes to print. I can share publicly how I feel about those older affirmations and the harm I now see they could do.

THE FORGIVENESS PRACTICE

Healing from shame, guilt, and *should haves* isn't often a quick fix. You can get clear with yourself and with the others involved, and then—*bam!*—something happens, or you flash back to a memory and instantly are taken over by shame, guilt, anger, and pain once again. I often say that grief is unpredictable, but I'd say the same for shame too. Even shame that you think that you have already healed from. You can't always know what will unearth it.

While I don't have a quick fix—like a *should* exorcism to make those feelings never arise again—I do have a practice that I utilize regularly that brings me right to my heart. It brings me healing, compassion, peace, and grounding.

I created this practice by accident a long time ago when I just couldn't get over how someone that I had thought of as a friend had acted. As much as I tried to make peace with the fact that her choices were her choices and it really wasn't my business, every time I heard her name or saw her, as she was a part of a large friend group, I would feel this inner rage. I felt she *should have* acted differently. She *should not have* done what she had done, and I couldn't get past it! After weeks of trying to let go and even having a clearing talk with her, I couldn't rid myself of my rage, and I found myself in the same place as her. I was sick of letting this person and something that I couldn't change take up so much of my mind space and emotional energy. I suddenly just started repeating to myself silently:

I forgive you. I forgive you. I forgive you. I forgive you.

I kept repeating it, and then magically I felt this intense energy that had a hold on me dissolve. It actually made me laugh, as I was like, Why am I forgiving her? Who am

"Sometimes you just don't know—until you know. Instead of beating yourself up for it, acknowledge yourself for seeing it now!"

I to be forgiving her? It doesn't even really have anything to do with me. She is a human, learning and growing by living, just like me. I do not want to be her best buddy. Why am I forgiving her?

It reminded me that forgiving someone has less to do with the other person and more to do with ourselves. Forgiveness is for us to be able to heal, move forward, and release the pain we are carrying. And it worked. There have been times since then with that same person and others that I feel triggered, and I bring myself right back to what I named my Forgiveness Practice. The practice is simply repeating "I forgive you" until I feel the energy dissipate. It may not rid you of it forever, but it is something to do in the moment that allows you to root down, release, and not be so reactive.

> Forgiving someone has less to do with the other person and more to do with ourselves. Forgiveness is for us to be able to heal, move forward, and release the pain we are carrying.

Just a few days after I accidentally created this practice in a restaurant in LA, I returned to my apartment in New York City so upset with myself for a money mismanagement. I left for my LA trip expecting a payment to come in the form of a direct deposit, and it never came. I went on my trip with only my debit card, and by the last two days there I was into negative numbers in my bank account. I couldn't pay for anything and had to borrow money from friends. I felt so irresponsible and much shame as I tallied the loans to pay them back. I had been fully paying my own way from the age of 19. I used to budget by the dollar to make sure I wasn't living beyond my means, and here I was at age 30 needing my friends to pay for my meals. I felt like such a failure to have to ask for support, especially financial support, even if I knew I would be able to pay them back within the next two weeks. I *should have* known better! I *should have* brought a credit card as a backup.

I just couldn't get over it. No matter how much I kept telling myself that it already happened, that I was supported, that my friends were happy to help, that I would learn from my money mismanaging, I just couldn't stop punishing myself. And then I started repeating to myself:

I forgive you. I forgive you. I forgive you. I forgive you.

I moved to the mirror and kept repeating it:

I forgive you. I forgive you. I forgive you. I forgive you.

Tears were streaming down my face as I kept repeating, "I forgive you." I sobbed and sobbed and kept repeating it until I felt myself surrender. Until I could feel myself healing and actually forgive myself.

It sounds too simple, I know. But we are often so busy analyzing, ruminating, and *should having* on ourselves that we just keep spinning instead of facing ourselves, working through it, and making space for healing. This Forgiveness Practice isn't a one-and-done practice, *but* when you catch yourself in the swirl of beating yourself up, feeling rage toward others, and *should having* your life away, please try to pause and try my Forgiveness Practice.

Say it, even right now; try it out. See how it feels to repeat it to yourself. Is there a *should have* that comes up for you right now? Say it in your mind, out loud, or really go for the full effect and stand in front of a mirror. (Using the selfie mode on your device will work too. Hey, maybe you can even record yourself saying it and play it back!)

I forgive you. I forgive you. I forgive you. I forgive you.

Say it until you can feel a shift in yourself. A release. Your heart opening. An exhale. A cry. You will know when you are good to stop. *And* this may be something you have to work up to. Sometimes we lock up our emotions (especially shame) so tightly that we are afraid to face them, to feel them, in order to release them.

You can also try writing it over and over again. But do yourself a favor and try it, and try it more than once, okay? It may not wipe the feelings away forever, but it will support you in the now and may allow you to move forward with more self-compassion and clarity. When the *should have* shame pops up another time, you can pull out our handy Forgiveness Practice again and again.

BABY STEP IT

Healing and forgiving takes time. Sometimes the pain may be too fresh to go straight to the Forgiveness Practice. That happened to me recently. As much as I wanted to heal and let go of the anger and *should have* pain that I was feeling, I was struggling to move through it. I tried saying, "I forgive you," but I just couldn't. The wound was too deep and too fresh. It felt like a lie, because it was. I was not in the place to be open to forgiveness yet, and that is okay. You can't force forgiveness. You can't force healing.

When I couldn't get "I forgive you" to come out of my mouth, there was a mantra that soothed and supported me:
It already happened.
It is not happening now.
I am here now.

In this instance, it had to do with another person that I could not yet bring myself to forgive, and what had happened felt like it had taken over my whole life. I couldn't stop thinking about it and how I felt this person *should have* acted, what they *should have* done, how they *should* be, how I *should have* responded, what I *should have* said and done, how I *should have* avoided this whole situation, and on and on. So I started repeating this:

I can't change what already happened.

I can't change other people.

I am letting go.

I am moving forward.

And then a little while later I was able to shift my energy slightly and started to repeat this when I thought of this person:

I am sending you peace.

I am sending you healing.

I tried again to attempt to say, "I forgive you" (just to myself, not to them), and it still felt too challenging for the level of pain, confusion, and anger I felt. So I said thank you instead.

Thank you.

Thank you for making me stronger.

Thank you for showing me your true colors.

Thank you for preparing me for obstacles to come.

This actually did help me to move through my anger and pain. It may sound ridiculous, but repeatedly thanking this person truly helped me move through my anger and pain, and it helped me laugh a bit too. Then, eventually, I did get to the Forgiveness Practice. The triggering didn't end. But it dulled. When I do get triggered, these are all mantras that help me to see my feelings, make space for them, and breathe through them. They support me in getting back to the present moment, to see the lessons, be compassionate with myself, and even have compassion for the other person (if there is one) and be able to keep showing up as the person I **want** to be.

STUDENT OF LIFE

One of my favorite quotes ever is:

> *The place where you are right now*
> *God circled on a map for you.*
>
> — HAFIZ

Even if you don't believe in God, or no matter what God you do believe in, doesn't that just feel like a sigh of relief? It cancels out all *should haves*! This place right here, with all the choices that you made, all the things you have said and done, were somehow a perfect part of your path. I mean, sometimes you just have to make three left turns, instead of one right turn, to get to where you want to go.

> Sometimes you just have to make three left turns, instead of one right turn, to get to where you want to go.

That is life. You live. You learn. That is how it works. And imagine how much more you see and learn by taking those three left turns. One of the first phrases that I had in my product line was "Student of Life." And that is another go-to mantra when you find yourself falling into *should haves*. To remind yourself:

I am a student of life.
I am living. I am learning. I am growing.

Instead of being haunted by your past, face it. Accept that it already happened. Instead of beating yourself up for what already happened, acknowledge your growth. Acknowledge that you are human. Acknowledge that you are learning. Receive yourself, and allow yourself to ground into the present moment, and set yourself up for the future you do **want**.

And remember this set of questions from the previous chapter:

- What am I feeling?
- Why?
- How do I want to feel?
- What can I do to support myself in feeling that right now?

This isn't to bypass any emotions, *but* to support you in bringing them to the surface, feeling through them, *and* making space for healing, joy, gratitude, forgiveness, and more.

"Instead of being haunted by your past, face it. Accept that it already happened. Instead of beating yourself up for what already happened, acknowledge your growth. Acknowledge that you are human. Acknowledge that you are learning."

CHAPTER 6

TRUST YOURSELF.

The reason that you have a hard time trusting your intuition is because you are convinced that some outside authority knows better than you.

—MARYAM HASNAA

It's time to talk about the elusive and ever-confusing intuition. What is it really, and how do you know when you are feeling it? Gut feelings can often feel murky and confusing because of the *shoulds* that fog up our connection to ourselves. Unshoulding yourself will create a direct line to your intuition.

I am someone who feels lucky to have felt a real connection to my intuition and to have trusted it from a young age. Yet it can still be incredibly difficult for me to figure out what my intuition is telling me. I'll wonder, *Is that my inner knowing, or is it a fear*? Does a feeling that I don't even fully understand and that does not always make sense really know what is right for me? Isn't it better to listen to people who know what they are talking about and have been there and done it themselves? I mean, what do I know? Besides myself? Do I even know myself?

How do you come to trust yourself if you are always looking outside of yourself for your answers? That's what the *shoulds* do: they have us looking outside of ourselves. Instead of trusting ourselves, we are conditioned to give power to outside voices over our own, and to model our lives, our appearance, our choices, after others. Which leads us to questioning, comparing, and outsourcing our life choices. I am not saying to never look outside of yourself or collect opinions, research, and feedback, *but* rather to allow your inner voice to be the guiding force in your life. Or to at least give it as much space and respect as you would give to any other expert. You are the expert on you. No one knows you better than you.

> That's what the *shoulds* do: they have us looking outside of ourselves. Instead of trusting ourselves, we are conditioned to give power to outside voices over our own, and to model our lives, our appearance, our choices, after others.

That is a powerful thought, right? That no one can ever possibly know *you* better than *you*. Not your parents, your siblings, your best friends whom you share everything with, your partner, your mentors, your boss. **No one will ever know you better than you know you.** It is the truth, and yet so often we don't even give ourselves a chance to be who we are, to trust who we are and what we feel, to allow ourselves to expand beyond who we were taught we *should* be. We are constantly evolving each day as we collect experiences, information, outside views, and shed the *shoulds* that life has imprinted on us. Your life belongs to you. Are you living it true to you?

Making friends with our intuition is so needed for big life stuff, but it is also so needed for our "little" everyday life choices. The ability to listen to and trust what we are feeling and allow ourselves to make the choices that work for us—without feeling shame, less than, or that we aren't doing it "right"—is so needed.

So, how do you uncover what it is that you feel—what works for you, what is best for you, what your gut is saying—when you are swimming in the thoughts, feelings, advice, and *shoulds* of others? How do you trust yourself when you are inundated with information about the best way to eat, take care of yourself, be productive, find your dream partner, etc., etc., etc.? Good question. Let's get into it!

JUST BECAUSE IT WORKS *FOR THEM*, IT DOESN'T MEAN IT IS *FOR YOU*

A few years back I bought a book from a home simplicity maven I admire in attempts to feel more organized and in control at home with two toddlers and a partner who was away for months at a time. In the book, she suggests doing a small load of laundry every single morning as the "simple" way to not be overwhelmed by laundry. Sounds simple enough! But when I read that, the idea of doing a load of laundry every single day felt overwhelming and stressful. Especially in the morning! I had enough things to do in the morning before I dropped off my kids at pre-school. But initially upon reading it, I felt like, well damn, this lady has an entire brand built on being organized. She has her shit together; maybe this is the way I *should* be doing laundry!

What works for her did not work for me. And that is perfectly perfect. I *love* how much access to information we have. I love that we can learn organization and house-keeping tips from people who have mastered it and have built successful businesses on it! I love that we can find reviews for every product, service, and technique. I love that we can learn from and see into the lives of people all around the world who are successful, knowledgeable, and vibrant. How lucky are we?

Yet at the same time, **having so much access to information can have us looking outside of ourselves more and more—instead of looking inside and trusting ourselves.** The access to information, suggestions, and how-tos creates more *shoulds* and comparison. It can make me question myself and how I do things and what feels best for me, because it seems like *everyone else* is doing it the way that *they* claim is the best.

When you allow yourself to lean in to your feelings and trust yourself, it will also support you in getting out of comparison and competitiveness. **What works for them doesn't have to be for you. What works for you doesn't have to be for them.** And that doesn't mean that anything is wrong with them and what they are doing or that there is anything wrong with you and what you are doing and how you do it! Instead of feeling shame for that or mulling over whose way is better and comparing yourself, honor it. Honor yourself.

COLLECTING DATA

I love getting feedback. I do listen to the opinions, suggestions, and experiences of others, but I make sure that I give my own thoughts and feelings just as much consideration. I think what often happens when we reach out, seek, and ask is that we forget that our opinions and feelings are valid, even if we have little to no experience with what we are exploring. We can be so busy looking for our answer outside of us that we forget that we matter too. And that is yet another gift of zeroing in on all the *shoulds*, whether the word itself is coming at you or simply the feeling.

When you find yourself asking for feedback, suggestions, and reviews, tell yourself that you are simply collecting data in order to make *your* choice. You aren't looking outside of yourself for your answer. You aren't looking for how you *should* do it or what you *should* do. You are researching, exploring, asking around to collect data in order to make the choice that feels best for *you*, and your life, right now.

Go ahead and gather opinions, do your research, read the reviews, and explore all the ways to do it. Setting yourself up this way will support you in exploring possibilities without making you feel like *they* know best, so you *should* do it their way. You know, the great *they*. They say the best way to launch a business is to follow these 5–10 proven steps. They say the key to locking in your ideal mate is by creating a clear list, and you will then manifest them into reality! They say the best foods to eat are this, not this, with a little of this, and make sure to watch that. . . Who the heck are *they*, and why are you listening to them and not *you* and how you feel and how your body responds?

Remember that no one knows you better than you. And also remember this about the data you collect, whether you get it directly from someone you know and trust, from someone who is the most successful version of what you envision for yourself, or a collection of blogs, reviews, etc. No one is exactly the same. Not all plans, five-step processes, ways of eating, top 10–rated items will work the same for each person. I mean, you could follow a step-by-step plan to a T, and that does not mean you will get the same results, even if you have a twin!

FEEL IT OUT—TRY IT ON

This is an idea that I got from my friend and podcast guest, Danika Brysha, co-founder and CEO of Model Meals and founder of Self-Care Society. I heard her talk about this idea of trying on careers and opportunities, just like you try on outfits. If it interests you, why not try it on? Instead of feeling like you have to make a choice and stick with it for the rest of your life, why not allow yourself to try on what calls to you? Just like you would try on different looks. Try on the job, try on the opportunity, and if it isn't for you, or you want to make another choice later, it isn't like you failed—you tried it on, and now you're ready to try on a different option. I loved the playfulness of this so much that it inspired how I talk about the visualization practice that I use to support me in making choices.

After you have collected your data, go through your options, lists, feedback, and possibilities, and visualize yourself trying the options on, just like how you would try on new clothes. Imagine you are in a dressing room, trying on different outfits. See yourself making these choices, doing the thing, buying the thing, spending time with the person—live it out in your mind, and try on how it feels for you. Do it playfully, allowing yourself to be creative, seeing your options as being flexible, not just automatically shooting yourself down, thinking, *Oh, I would never. That is not for me. That will never work for me.* Sometimes giving myself the space to visualize multiple scenarios, including the ones I feel like are a no, makes me lean in and consider others, and also what good could come from them, instead of just doing what sounds easiest, most common, most acceptable—the option I feel I *should* choose.

What do you feel? What fears, doubts, worries surface? Do you feel excited, comfortable, playful, lit up? Do you feel tense, stressed, uncomfortable, insecure? Be real with yourself while also allowing yourself to explore and daydream. Listen to the tugs, nudges, and feelings that are poking you outside of your comfort zone. Do you feel like your gut is saying *yes*, but you have some nagging tugs and/or questions? Try journaling about the visualizations or describing them to someone to really try them on. Does it feel exciting, even if there are fears poking at you? What is the main energy that you feel? You don't have to even name it, but feel into that baseline energy. Try on the possibilities, and allow yourself to get quiet and lean toward the inner pulling.

Once you have tried on the possibilities and envisioned yourself making the different choices—whether it is which stroller to buy, how to start a new business, or when to end a relationship—you may already be clear on what you are feeling and what is your true gut **want**. Awesome! If not—or if you want to double-check and reinforce that feeling—ask yourself some more questions. You don't need to answer all of them, but scan through and give yourself a check-in.

> **Self-Inquiry Questions**
> - Does this feel more like a *should* or a **want**?
> - What is motivating my choice?
> - Am I making this choice out of fear, doubt, and/or concern of what someone else will think?
> - How does it make me feel to make this choice?
> - When I get quiet and let all the other voices and *shoulds* fall away, what feels best to me?

IS IT MY INTUITION TALKING OR MY FEARS?

One question that I often hear (and can still feel myself sometimes) is how to tell the difference between a gut feeling that is your intuition tugging at you versus a fear that is holding you back. It can often be confusing. You would think your intuition is like this clear ringing bell with a giant spotlight saying, "It's this way. Follow me!" Making it all lit up, clear, and easy to listen to. And it's often not. It is often murky, because we have layers of *shoulds* and data to wade through.

Sometimes what we think is our initial gut reaction is actually a fear, doubt, or limiting belief. These feelings can cause us to freeze up or react immediately. But if you allow yourself to dig in, to get curious, to visually try it on and feel your way through it, you will be able to uncover whether it is your intuition talking or your fear. Some things that show up as big no's right away may be things you do **want** to question and try on. Maybe they are just out of your comfort zone, maybe they are too far away from what you have been led to believe you *should* do, or maybe they really are not for you.

When I allow myself to try on an idea and it kind of feels too big, too hard, too far away for me, *yet* I can feel something pulling me toward it, some deep-down butterflies of excitement, some curiosity. I trust those deeper feelings and remind myself of what I talked about in Chapter 3 about how having a fear is more work than diving into it.

You can and likely will feel more than one thing at once. I will often feel both scared and excited. But underneath the fear, I can tell that the excitement is pulling me there to trust myself to lean toward the **want**. Both fears and your intuition can feel like an anxious tugging energy. When you feel deeper into it, you can make space to feel into the nervousness, fears, and more. Even with this anxious energy, you can truly feel your intuition in your center, your core, your gut. Whereas fears can feel more like a poking, a constriction, a clenching in the shoulders, neck, stomach. Gut feelings may not make sense, they may not have an explanation to go with them, but you can just feel their solidness and simplicity. Fears, doubts, and worries, on the other hand, can hand you a 500-page book to try to convince you to listen to them. It can be scary, it can be uncomfortable, but you can trust yourself and what you feel.

And if you still don't know what you feel and what to trust, look to your values. Which choice feels most aligned with your values and what you value?

YOUR INTUITION MAY PISS YOU OFF

I remember when we were living in the time when COVID was just starting to be a thing—remember March 2020? It was early on, so we didn't really know what it was and how serious it was. We saw that countries like Italy went on total lockdown, but in the USA, it still felt like, huh? Seriously? It can't be that bad. Things hadn't fully shut down yet, and so we were left to make the choices ourselves. My kids' preschool never shut down. I really didn't want them home with me, because how would I get any work done? *Should* I send them or not? I remember a friend who is a yoga teacher was wondering if she *should* cancel her classes. There were so many unknowns that could last for months or years. I was torn. Do I keep my kids home even though I have paid for the month and the school is staying open? I really didn't want to; I was committed to a major project I was working on. I asked friends locally and in other cities what they were doing. I just really didn't know. Then I got quiet, and even though I really **wanted** to have my work hours, especially since I was nearing the finish line with this *huge* project I had dreamed of my entire life, I felt deep inside that what was best was keeping them home.

I really, really, really **wanted** to keep sending them to school, but inside I felt this inner pull that I kind of **wanted** to ignore. Sometimes you just have to trust that deeper feeling within, even if you don't like what it is telling you. Even when it pisses you off. Even when it feels easier to not listen to it. I kept them home, my huge project got delayed for several months, and yet the timing ended up working for the best. The delay actually ended up being beneficial to the project, and I felt good about my choice for many reasons, even though it pissed me off at the time.

What I want to be clear about is that trusting your gut, letting your intuition guide you, listening to your inner knowing, will not always be easy. It will not always feel like this magical force lighting you up, or like a—ding! ding! ding!—game show bell that goes off when you feel it and go with it. Honestly, it's often really fucking confusing. You can trust the deeper feelings within, you can trust your gut, you can trust you, even when you don't fully understand it all.

> Sometimes you just have to trust that feeling inside, even if you don't like what it is telling you. Trusting your gut, letting your intuition guide you, listening to your inner knowing, will not always be easy.

Sometimes, you don't know *how* you know, but you know that you know. Sometimes even when you make the choice and you do trust yourself, you may feel shaky for a while after, still doubting if you did indeed make the best choice. And then other times, as soon as you listen to yourself, you feel like you instantly dropped a shit ton of baggage and you could leap over buildings, and you start dancing in the street because you just know.

I don't know for sure, but I have to believe that the reason that connecting with ourselves and trusting what we feel can be so damn hard is because of the *should* world we live in. Most of us were not taught to question what is and to trust ourselves. I was shocked recently when I talked to a dear friend who felt her entire life that she had been programmed to trust anyone *but* herself. We do grow and evolve from other people's lessons, wisdom, and experiences, but we also need to stop discounting ourselves and what we feel and **want**.

STOP TRYING TO FORCE WHAT DOESN'T FIT/WORK

When I quit touring and fully committed to creating a business and being a coach, I felt such a sense of empowerment and freedom. I got to make my own hours! I got to choose what I offered and how I served and for how much! I was creating my own path! I got to work from my couch in leggings or write in my hammock! But at the same time, I started to question and sabotage myself. I struggled to allow myself true freedom at first, because I was getting caught in some *shoulds* based on comparison. I felt that I *should* be working by 9 A.M. every day. I felt I *shouldn't* work nights or weekends, as I needed to create work/life balance, after seeing other solopreneurs talk about and create their own boundaries. Here I was, free to do things my way but feeling wrong for doing what worked for me, and that just sucked.

I gave myself a good F the *Shoulds* pep talk and reminded myself that if taking the first half of the day for myself and starting to work at 2 P.M. and into the evening worked for me, *great*! Even though a part of me wished I was able to go to sleep early and wake up early, when I allowed myself to go with what was actually working best for me, instead of trying to fit myself into a *should* schedule, I found true productivity, creativity, and freedom! Over the years, as my life and family have shifted and changed, so has my approach to my work hours. Sometimes that means having weekend boundaries; sometimes it means I get my best work done on the weekends. And it's all perfect, because it is what works for me!

If you work best in the evening and you can, great! If you like to wake up at 4 A.M. to write and that works for you, great! If you are not a morning person, great! Stop making yourself wrong for what works for you. Where in your life are you forcing what doesn't fit? Maybe it used to, and you have outgrown it. Maybe it never really was for you, but you adapted to it because you were following unconscious or conscious *shoulds*. Allow yourself to be yourself. Allow yourself to trust yourself. Allow yourself to listen to yourself. Stop making it harder than it needs to be!

SOCIETAL NORMS DON'T HAVE TO BE YOUR NORMS

At the time of writing this book, I made the major life call to act on what I had been feeling for a long time and to re-create the relationship I have with my children's father. We never got married, but to the outside world, that is how we appeared—people always called him my husband. I love him. I am so glad that he is the father of my children, and we will always be family. But that doesn't mean that we have to live in the same home and continue with the same relationship we started with. I know having parents in separate homes will bring challenges for my children, but I also personally know the challenges of living in a home with two parents who are committed to staying together for their kids, even though it affects their own happiness and joy for life.

We are all led to believe that we *should* stay together for the kids, that we *should* be committed to working it out, especially if there isn't a clear issue like abuse, cheating,

"Stop making yourself wrong for what works for you. Allow yourself to be yourself. Allow yourself to trust yourself. Allow yourself to listen to yourself."

or addiction. My relationship wasn't "bad," but it didn't feel great. It wasn't a relationship that I thrived in. We get to reinvent our relationships. We get to reinvent our lives. And it doesn't have to make sense to anyone but us. We are still a family, and we get to define what that looks like over and over again. There is so much shame projected onto people for being single or divorced, but *why*? Like seriously, *why*? Your relationship status has nothing to do with your worth. You aren't failing at life or partnerships or love. So many people, when they heard about our relationship transition, told me, "I'm so sorry." And I replied with, "Why are you sorry? You don't need to be sorry. You can congratulate me for making the choices that are for my family's best interests. I feel great about my choices."

Please allow yourself to thrive in your life by trusting yourself, how you feel, who you are, and what you **want**.

YOU ARE THE AUTHORITY OF YOUR LIFE

I am the authority on my life. You are the authority on your life. And that means that you get to make the choices that feel aligned to you. That means you are free to change your mind. And you get to do this without feeling shame or guilt or any weirdness. Let me say it again. You, and only you, are the authority on you and your life. Not the people who raised you and love you deeply, not your best and oldest friends, not your boss, not your mentor, not your biggest cheerleaders and fans, not your partner. No one knows you better than you. And let's just be clear that we are always learning, growing, and evolving—so you will also constantly be learning about you! But you can be learning about *you* and still be the authority on *you*.

So, when the swirling *should* confusion starts to bubble up inside of you and you are feeling pulled in different directions of what to do, what choice to make, wondering if you are making the "right" choice—come back to yourself, remind yourself, and repeat to yourself:

I am the authority on my life.

I allow myself to trust what I feel.

I allow myself to trust myself.

You are not under obligation to offer up an explanation or to take on anyone else's confused, unsettled, or "I know better" vibes that may come at you. You can be confident in your choices, even when you don't have solid data to explain the why behind your choice. Because it feels right, or is best for you, is reason enough. Other people's opinions, experiences, and research don't have to be the guiding force of your life (except maybe in life-or-death situations and global pandemics).

Keep reminding yourself that even if someone else has a shit ton more experience with something, you have a shit ton more experience with *you*! And also think about the variety of people who have made big things happen. Most of them did *not* follow a "you *should* do *xyz*, proven five-step process" to make it. They did it their way. Allow yourself to do it your way. Listen to yourself. Trust yourself. You are the authority on you, and you will always be evolving.

Your life is yours, and you are the one who has to live with yourself and your choices each day. So try things on and out. Trust yourself. Change your mind. Changing your mind doesn't make you wishy-washy or distrustful; it shows you are seeking, growing, and aware. And remember that those things you might think are "mistakes" or "failures" are just learning. So if you make a choice where you went against your gut and then it didn't work out and you want to get all "Damn it, I *should have* trusted that feeling! But I trusted this person because they really seemed to know what they are talking about. Or everyone was doing it, so I thought, I *should* . . ." It's all learning!

Come back to yourself with compassion, and add that experience to your memory bank for future reference when you start talking yourself out of what you **want** and are afraid to trust yourself because it feels, scary, confusing, or lonely.

In case no one told you:

Trusting your intuition
can feel annoying,
can feel scary,
can feel lonely,
can feel confusing,
but it is always, always,
always worth it.

CHAPTER 7

WHAT WILL THIS MEAN ABOUT ME?—THE FEAR OF BEING JUDGED.

So much of our lives are driven and dictated by the fear of being judged. This fear is one of the biggest things that holds us back and robs us of our joy. I noticed that whenever I would fumble between a *should* versus a **want**, it was because there was this concern deep down about what other people will think about me or judge me for. Unknowingly, we often make what we assume other people *may* think about us to be more valuable than our own opinion of ourselves.

> We often make what we assume other people *may* think about us to be more valuable than our own opinion of ourselves.

Even to this day, after having laser focus on *shoulds* for over a decade, I regularly find I have to pull myself out of the deep depths of worries and doubts that come from the fear of being judged and what others will/do think about me. The good news is that I am now able to uncover these feelings and expose them for what they are so that I can get back to what really matters, and you will be able to now too!

Years ago, when I was preparing to launch my first professionally designed website, I learned one of the biggest lessons of my life. I was living in New York City at the time and had planned out a photoshoot with an uber-talented photographer, Brett, who was a friend of mine. I was so freaking excited. I had made up these handwritten cardboard signs to hold up in the photos saying things like, "What You Want, Wants You" and "Fuck Your Fears." I had a couple of fun outfits packed to wear with these metallic high-tops I loved. I took more time than I normally did to do my hair and makeup as I prepared for the shoot. The vision I had of standing in the streets of New York City holding my signs was about to come true!

I was about to leave to meet Brett, when I snapped into the reality that I would be posing as the obvious subject of a photoshoot out on the hip downtown streets with a pro photographer and a giant light-reflecting thingy (you know those big, white, umbrella-like things) aimed at me. *Oh shit. What are people going to think when they see me having my photo taken? Who is that girl? Why is she having photos taken? She obviously isn't important. She isn't thin enough or pretty enough or cool enough to have her photo taken.* In an instant, all of these judgments were being thrown at me.

And then I realized, I was still standing alone in my apartment.

All of those judgmental thoughts that had gone through my mind—all of those worries of what everyone would be thinking about me—were my own thoughts. My own inner judgments had taken over. I was suddenly faced with these very real beliefs that existed within me—that I was not worthy of having my photo taken on the NYC streets. I saw crystal clear for the first time that the judgments that I worried other people may have of me were actually my own! They were thoughts, beliefs, judgments that existed within me. *Damn.*

Acknowledging that those were my own judgments was heartbreaking. It was easier to live in a world where I believed that I was secure in myself and that it was just the messed-up world that judged me for my size, outfit choices, messy hair, imperfect skin, and more. I had been clinging to the belief that I loved myself ever since I chose to live at 15. And it was true. I did love myself. But I wasn't being honest about and facing the very real, judgmental thoughts that I had about myself that were not so loving. Beliefs about how I *should* look and be that had formed at a young age, when I was told I was fat as a child. From then on I had been comparing myself to other people that the world idolized for their thinness and beauty. I had internalized the belief that my worth was tied to how my body looked.

When I turned the tables on myself and saw that what I was afraid other people would judge me for were actually my own inner judgments of myself, it sucked. But it was also such a life-changing, slap-in-the-face wake-up call. Now that I saw that a part of me still believed those things, that I felt that I wasn't enough because my external appearance didn't fit into some unreal standard, I was able to face those fucked-up beliefs. Now that I had acknowledged and faced my inner judgments, I got to question them.

Is that really what I believe?

I wish I could tell you that I didn't, but yes, a part of me unfortunately believed and can still struggle with these not-enough beliefs that are tied to my external appearance. And that is due to all the *shoulds* that are embedded in us. The *shoulds* start to become part of our own beliefs, and it sucks. But! We are not stuck with our initial thoughts, feelings, and judgments. We can question them!

> We are not stuck with our initial thoughts, feelings, and judgments. We can question them!

So yes, a part of me really felt less than—like I wasn't beautiful enough, important enough, interesting enough, thin enough to have my photo taken—because that was the message I had received from the media. I did not fit the mold that I was sold. But I was able to question these beliefs. Did I really **want** to believe that? Did I really **want** to believe that I was not worthy of having photos taken for a website where I would be empowering people to own who they are and take their lives and minds into their own hands?

Fuck, no! I didn't **want** to believe that! So I asked myself:

Is that really what I want to believe about myself?

What do I want to believe?

I **want** to believe that even though I am not stick thin like the supermodels I grew up admiring, I am completely worthy of being seen, of being heard, of sharing my voice and using my own face and body as they are to represent myself and my mission.

And just that—just by being honest with myself and going beneath the programming that has been layered onto me by the diet obsessed world I grew up in to ask myself, "What do I **want** to believe?"—I opened up space for a new reality, for an expansion of my beliefs, and I gave myself a new life motto.

From that day forward, I carried around with me the mantra of "The Only Judge of Me, Is Me" to remind me that what matters most is what I believe to be true about myself and to keep coming back to these questions when the "What will they think?" worries arise.

What am I telling myself?

Do I believe that?/Do I want to believe that?

What do I want to believe?

"The Only Judge of Me, Is Me" reminds me to stop worrying about what others may or may not think about me and to keep coming back to: What do I think about me? What do I believe about me? Why do we put so much weight on what others think and so little weight on what we think about ourselves?

> Why do we put so much weight on what others think and so little weight on what we think about ourselves?

The fear of being judged is actually a mask for the judgments we have of ourselves. When you see that it is actually your own *shoulds* and judgments of yourself that are holding you back, you can begin to question, move through, and heal those judgments.

A JUDGMENT CAN HAVE POWER OVER YOU ONLY YOU IF YOU BELIEVE IT TO BE TRUE

Even though I had that breakthrough moment on the day of the NYC photoshoot and had even created products branded with my new favorite mantra, I of course was not completely cured of the fear of being judged. I had become way more present to when I was creating judgments of myself so that I could call them out, but this next realization I had years later felt even more groundbreaking to me. And every time that I share it with others, I get asked to repeat it over and over again so that they can let the power of it settle within them.

As someone with a chronic invisible illness, I learned to heal a lot of my daily pains by focusing on nutrition and taking care of my body. I gave up gluten in 2004, and it helped me so much that I never went back. I was mostly vegan for a good stretch but never completely. When I became pregnant, I craved red meat and found even after giving birth that my body felt good having it in my life sometimes. Yet I carried around some remnant of shame about eating a hamburger and french fries. That wasn't healthy! When a new burger chain opened up near me that promoted grass-fed beef and offered gluten-free buns, I tried it out and fell in love. It felt like a fun treat, and it became one of my favorite meals to eat out. When I found myself home for most of the year with two toddlers while their dad was on tour, I started a routine of going to this burger spot on Mondays because kids ate free! You gotta love a deal!

I was stoked for our weekly meal out—no cooking or clean-up for me and a treat of a meal that I couldn't make at home. In those first weeks of this new fun tradition, I savored every bite but also felt pangs of guilt, shame, and judgment. I felt like everyone there was judging me because my two- and four-year-old were having cheeseburgers and fries and (organic) chocolate milk for dinner. Here I was, trying to enjoy this treat of a meal and feeling like I was a bad mother for it.

I struggled to shake off these shitty feelings. I mean, I was doing something I wanted to do! I felt great about my choice! Or did I? Who is doing the judging right now, Tricia, them or you? Me. It was me. I was judging myself for the choices I was making. So, while I really wanted to be enjoying the meal that I was excited about, that I wanted, I was shaming myself for it. A past dream version of me who envisioned my children only eating wonderful, homemade organic food, with a fruit and veggie at every meal, with their diverse, advanced palates, was judging this very real me. *Ugh!*

I mean, how ridiculous that I was worried about being judged by the same people at the same restaurant, eating the same food. I mean, really, how inventive are our minds and the stories they create? I was the one who felt that I was not a good mom for feeding my kids a hamburger and fries. But I was projecting it onto others, assuming that it was what they must have thought about me. I had to get real with myself, my thoughts, my beliefs, and my inner judgments. I had to call myself out on them and hold them under a microscope to see what my actual feelings were.

I realized in that moment that a judgment can only have power over me if it is something that I believe to be true. So I asked myself, "Tricia, do you really, truly believe that you are not a good mother because your kids are eating a hamburger and fries? I mean, seriously? Do you?" No, I don't. I mean, that is ridiculous. I know that I am an amazing mother. Once I got real with myself and clarified my feelings and questioned my fears of being judged, I felt all the tension fade away.

This aha thought has become my new constant check-in when I feel myself in the discomfort, the fear, the heaviness, the looming dread that come with the worry of being judged and also when I am truly being judged by someone else.

When I remind myself of this, it makes me look deeper and face the judgment to ask myself the questions that came up for me all of those years ago before the photoshoot:

Is that really what I believe?

What do I want to believe?

Asking yourself these questions creates an immediate reality check. Because yes, judgment is real. Our brains are naturally wired to take in information and interpret it. Our brains are naturally wired to create judgments. So judgments are going to keep coming at us, from inside of us and outside of us. Other people will judge you. No matter what you eat, what you do, look like, say, etc., and that sucks. It really does. But I have found that often times it is our own judgments of ourselves that weigh us down and hold us back the most.

"A judgment can have power over you only if it is something that you believe to be true."

Anytime that you find yourself stuck in the fear of what will "they" think, anytime that you truly are being judged, anytime you catch yourself judging yourself, remind yourself: a judgment can only have power over you if you believe it to be true.

Do you believe it to be true?

THE FEAR OF BEING JUDGED HAS US QUESTIONING OUR WANTS

This may sound silly to you, but this was something I truly felt shame around a couple of years ago. I have always loved to read. I remember being a kid and reading a book a day on some summer days at home. My love of reading picked back up once I was living on tour buses and airplanes crisscrossing the globe. I loved to read biographies, memoirs, and novels, and always had a few on me. (Thank goodness digital books and e-readers now make for much lighter travel bags!)

When I started to become part of the personal development and wellness world with my brand Your Joyologist, I noticed that I was afraid to admit that I read novels. I would tell people I forgot what I was reading or what the last book I read was when they asked. I would hide the books so no one would see them. I didn't even allow myself to read them for a while. What will it mean about me if people know that I love to devour novels? Including light, beach-read, romance novels!

What was happening was an internal judgment. I was ashamed that I was reading novels and not books that were meant to give me knowledge and growth. I felt that I *should* be reading all the newest and oldest self-help and educational books. I *should* only be doing wellnessy, self-improvement things. I *should* be doing something more productive with my time. I *should* be doing something "better."

The *shoulds* will have us judging ourselves for our **wants**, for what brings us joy, for what nurtures us. They make us afraid to own our **wants**, what makes us come alive, what serves and nurtures us, for fear of being judged. For fear of what will it mean about us, but here is the thing:

> **What matters most is what I believe to be true about me.**
>
> **What matters most is what you believe to be true about you.**

So, when I feel shame, when I can feel this pressure or this "what if they find out" feeling, this "what will this mean about me" feeling, I get to ask myself, "Well, Tricia, what do you believe that this means about you?" I get to look deeper.

Do you believe that reading novels is a waste of your time? Do you believe that because you read novels you must not have anything wise to say?

Do you believe that people who want to support others are only allowed to be growing, learning, and sharing and are not allowed to do anything that entertains and nurtures them?

No, no, no, I don't! I love to read novels! For me it is a major act of self-care and relaxation to fully immerse myself in a novel, because I cannot multitask while doing it, and my brain gets to shut off from working, developing, and creating. And these fictional stories are often entertaining, enriching, and educational because they open me up to a broader experience of life.

If we don't question these feelings of what we *should* and *should not* be doing, we end up living with shame, fears, and inner judgment from even the smallest of life choices. Also, in the questioning, you may get clear about a change you do **want** to make, a habit that you do **want** to stop, a place where you do **want** to try on and make space for different possibilities, and it will be coming from *you*. Instead of from a place of thinking about what others will think about you, it will come from what you **want** for you. For instance, I could have decided that, yes, I love to read novels *and* I want to make space to read more educational books. Ask yourself:

What do I believe this means about me?

What do I want for myself?

What are my own inner judgments keeping me from doing?

THIS IS YOUR PERMISSION SLIP

A past client of mine had no fear about saying she loves *NSYNC or Justin Timberlake when she was growing up and into her teen years. It was fun music that brought her joy. But when she got into her 20s Emily felt like she would be judged by her peers or society at large for still liking that music. She felt that she *should* like other music, like eclectic acoustic singer-songwriters. She wasn't allowing herself to simply love the music that she loved because she felt like "I wasn't allowed." When *NSYNC got its star on the

Hollywood Walk of Fame in 2018, she left work to attend, since she worked nearby. She told everyone at work where she was going and even said to her therapist, "I don't care what they think. I am who I am. I love *NSYNC! I'm not going to miss this opportunity," but even still—inside she was judging herself for going. Even though there were over 2,500 fans on Hollywood Boulevard to see *NSYNC get their star, she still judged herself for going.

It wasn't until two years later when she discovered an *NSYNC podcast called *Girl, Were You Alone?* that she let go of that inner judgment. In the first episode, the co-host Ashley said, "You can be a grown-ass woman, you can pay your bills, you can have your relationships and friendships and hobbies and do whatever you want, and you can still be completely obsessed with a boy band from twenty years ago. It's fine; do your thing," and she thought to herself, *Yes, finally! Permission!* It felt like she needed that permission to go back into full swing loving them.

> *I felt so much freer for myself to love *NSYNC—and do whatever I want, really! I became more accepting of others, and it really helped lighten space up on my end. Because I let myself off the hook for "secretly loving a music group that hasn't put out new music in 20 years," I let others off the hook too. By the co-hosts simply just being themselves, they allowed me, and all of us who listen, to continue being ourselves. To just live our lives and like what we like and not feel alone or judge ourselves for it!*

I *love* that story so much and was so freaking happy for her and proud of her when she had that moment. Again, this is something that may seem small, but she was constantly bearing the weight of her own judgments and not allowing herself to enjoy what she enjoys for *years*. The small stuff matters.

Where are you robbing yourself of joy for the fear of being judged because you are stuck in a *should* story? Where are you hiding part of yourself or something that brings you joy for fear that someone else won't accept you? In doing that you are not accepting you.

Set yourself free! Allow yourself to do what lights you up, fulfills you, nurtures you—what brings *you* joy. And as Emily said, it won't just affect you! Owning your joy, claiming your wants, dropping your own inner judgment, will give permission to others to do the same! By giving yourself a permission slip to be who you are fully, you will also be granting a permission slip to others for them to own who they are fully.

WHY WE JUDGE

Oftentimes when we are living into the fear of being judged, we end up judging others. Think about it. Can you think of someone who often judges you or comes off as judgmental toward you or others? If you can't think of someone, let's just talk about mothers and mom shaming, because it is the freaking worst and it makes no sense. Like, being a mom is a lot. Why the hell are we ripping people apart and not showing all the compassion in the world? It mystifies me, but this is what I came up with in trying to understand it.

When someone makes a different choice than us, something in our brain jumps to believing there is a right and a wrong. So, if I choose option A and they choose option B, they automatically go into defensive mode, thinking I may be judging them for choosing "wrong." So they judge me so that they can deflect feeling "wrong."

Does that seem ridiculous to you? Does it also kind of make sense? I am not saying it is right! But I think that is what we often do without realizing it. It's an ignorant-ass form of self-defense. Instead of just being able to agree to disagree or to agree that different things and ways work for different people/kids/families/times, people are afraid of being judged "wrong"—so they judge to feel they are "right." So that they can feel at peace with their own choices.

Seeing this is another way that I can come back to myself when I am in a space of judgment, whether someone else is judging me or I can feel myself judging them. It allows me to pull myself back from the judgments or fear of being judged and come from a space of acceptance and compassion. My choices are my choices. Their choices are their choices.

> My choices are my choices. Their choices are their choices.

When you catch yourself judging someone else, come back to you. What are you really feeling? What are you needing? What are you worried about being judged for? Are you looking for approval? What is really happening? And when you find yourself being judged by someone else, give yourself love and compassion, ask yourself, "What do I believe?" and try to hold any amount of compassion for the other person/people, as it may very well be some sort of self-defense on their part that has them projecting judgment onto you.

CHAPTER 8

QUIT QUESTIONING YOUR ENOUGH-NESS.

A month before I graduated college, I moved across the country to live in San Diego to start working for a top touring sound company and was delighted when a few months later my college besties moved from Chicago to Los Angeles. We may have had a few hours between us, but I was ecstatic to have my friends somewhat close by, and on every rare weekend that I had off from working concerts, I went up to LA to have fun with them. My friends loved the up-and-coming (at the time) hipster eastside neighborhoods of Silver Lake and Echo Park. They loved going to the hip brunch spots and coffee shops. Meanwhile, I hated that area of town. I felt like everybody was dressed like they were too cool for school, with unique hair styles, vintage clothes, and more. Everyone there appeared to me to be confident and cool, and I felt like an outsider. I felt like everyone was looking at me and judging my non-cool clothes, non-stick-thin body, not-done-up face and hair. I *never* felt comfortable there.

Once I chose to eliminate *shoulds* from my life, I saw that the reason that I felt so uncomfortable and self-conscious in the many diverse neighborhoods in LA was not because everyone else was judging me and looking down on me. It was because I never felt like I was enough. Honestly, I felt out of place all over LA, from Venice to Beverly Hills to Downtown. I felt like an outsider. I felt less than.

Even though I was not sitting around telling myself these things, it was so embedded into my psyche that it became a subconscious truth that I lived into. I had always been someone who was pretty self-confident. I mean, I really felt like I was a badass working in the rock-and-roll business as one of the very few female sound engineers. In that atmosphere I stood out and felt good about myself. Yet when I was out in the "real" world, I constantly struggled with my enough-ness.

The *shoulds* that we absorb and take on put us into constant comparison, and it is so soul-killing and gross. I don't even like using the word *gross*, but really, it is. Why, oh why must we be constantly questioning our worth and comparing ourselves to others? Why can't we just surrender to our innate enough-ness!

Once I was able to start calling bullshit on my own thoughts and beliefs, I ended up loving LA and even moved to Echo Park myself. I was able to feel confident, at ease, and at home in my body and my surroundings, walking around in my workout clothes, with no makeup and messy hair in the hipster areas and the ritzy areas. Enough-ness is not something that is obtained with the approval of others; it is within us, and it is available to us at all times. We just have to allow ourselves to access it.

"Enough-ness is not something that is obtained with the approval of others— it is within us, and it is available to us at all times. We just have to allow ourselves to access it."

~~IF/THEN~~—F THAT. I AM ENOUGH, RIGHT NOW!

When I got booked for my first speaking gig after having kids and then putting my work in the backseat for a couple of years, I was so honored, excited, and nervous. It had been at least four years since I stood in front of people with all eyes on me. I spent so much time thoughtfully preparing my speech, practicing it and fine tuning it so that it would have the biggest impact. The speech was focused on what I talked about in the previous chapter: our own inner judgment and how to call it out, heal it, and move beyond it.

When it got to the week before the talk, I became overwhelmed with a laundry list of external things that I felt I had to do in order to prepare for being on stage. Really, I was confronted with a bunch of *shoulds* that took me a little while to unravel. I felt pressure that I *should* exercise every day that week so that I would appear thinner and fitter when I was standing on stage. I *should* go shopping for a much cooler outfit than what I owned to look more interesting to the audience. I *should* go get a gel manicure so that I appeared put together and professional. I even felt that I *should* get my car washed and detailed, even though it was likely that not a single person attending would see my car! To be clear, in my mind I didn't use the word *should*, but the energy was there tallying up these to-dos.

I just wanted to do the real preparation work, practicing in front of people and seeing how I did without using note cards, keeping it engaging and not feeling word-for-word rehearsed. But my focus kept getting distracted by the building pressures of these invisible *shoulds*.

It would be one thing if I actually enjoyed sitting in a nail salon and getting my nails done or wandering through racks of clothes to pick a new outfit. If those were things that brought me joy and felt empowering or relaxing to me, it would be a slightly different story, but they didn't. I mean, I love good clothes and I love the look of my nails being done, *but* the shopping and sitting are not ways that I enjoy spending time. They make me itchy and anxious, and I also didn't have money to throw around at the time. The time and expenses of getting a new outfit, manicure, blowout, and car wash felt stressful and overwhelming to me. So why did I keep feeling like I *had* to do it all?

By getting present to my anxious, stressed feelings and actually naming them and exploring what I was really feeling, I was able to unravel these *shoulds* that I was feeling. I was able to see what it was that I **wanted** and where these thoughts and feelings were coming from. At the root of all of those *shoulds* was that I felt that *if* I slimmed down (like how much would I really slim down in a week, anyway) and had a cool outfit and cool nails, *then* the people in the audience would believe I was worthy of being a speaker. Subconsciously, I was telling myself that what I had to say wasn't important enough, that my story and message wouldn't be impactful *unless* I looked the part of what I have been sold into believing a public speaker *should* look like.

It's such bullshit! Empowering speakers come in all shapes and sizes. They wear everything from jeans and T-shirts to bold outfits, to business suits, to flowy dresses, to activewear with running shoes. I had to get clear with myself that while I was wanting to impact the people in the audience with my message, I was also craving for them to accept me. I was looking for the people in that room to tell me that I was enough. To tell me that I was worthy of being seen and heard. Even though I had been asked to speak there, even though I really believed I had something powerful to share, I was so deeply struggling with not being enough.

I was afraid of being rejected, but what I was doing was rejecting myself. I was telling myself that I was not enough unless I looked a certain way on the outside. I was distracting myself from sharing the life-changing message of calling out our inner judge—by judging myself! So I had to apply the very work of the speech on myself in preparation for the speech.

Shoulds cloud our feelings of enough-ness, and it is such crap. I kept getting stuck into the trap of *if* I do *xyz*, *then* people will take me seriously. *If* I look the part, *then* I will appear worthy of being on this stage, of being heard, of being seen. *If* I look the part, *then* people will see me, accept me, love me, validate me.

When, really, those external things have little to do with my self-worth, my purpose, my story. Sure, looking presentable is desirable and could give me more confidence. I mean, I am all for expressing ourselves via our wardrobes and having, as my friend and public speaking coach Jacki Carr says, a "power outfit" that supports us in feeling our most badass selves. But I was allowing the *shoulds* that society puts on us to question myself and if I was worthy of sharing my message. When at the end of the day, it isn't going to matter what I wore, what my weight was, if I had a blowout, if my nails were done, and if I got my car washed. What matters is what I say and believe, and how I present it so that it lands with the audience. I could have the best outfit, body, nails, hair, and car in town, but if I am pinning my enough-ness on those external things, I will never truly feel enough, worthy, or validated.

The *shoulds* have us constantly doubting our self-worth and our enough-ness! They keep us looking for validation outside of ourselves, and even when we get it, we won't truly feel it unless we validate ourselves. Call out those *shoulds* and see them for the bullshit that they are. Allow yourself to validate yourself.

What bullshit "if/then" stories have you been living into and believing? If you keep putting your worth outside of yourself, you will keep chasing it, no matter how many goal marks you hit.

> Allow yourself to validate yourself.

FLEXING YOUR SELF-WORTH MUSCLE

One thing I still struggle with is believing that I have just as much worth as the people I look up to and admire—even if those people are my friends. A big memory I have of confronting this was a time I was on a tour break (this was after giving up the *shoulds* and re-creating myself as a touring Joyologist). I chose to spend a few days in LA to visit my favorite spots and see friends. I put the word out that I would be in town and started to make plans. One e-mail that I sent was to a newer friend, someone whom I had long admired and had happened to meet a few years prior, but due to both of us traveling, hadn't spent much time with. This man is an impressive triathlete who has founded and been a part of several successful companies, written three books, and is always up to something exciting and groundbreaking. I was a bit nervous around him because of all his success.

I pushed my fears, doubts, and expectations of getting a no aside and sent an e-mail asking if he wanted to meet up that week. I was over-the-moon excited when he said *yes*! Holy shit! He said yes! The only thing was that he suggested meeting for lunch in Santa Monica on Wednesday, and I was staying all the way across town and already had plans to be on the Westside on Thursday. If you are familiar with LA traffic, you understand the cloud hanging over my excitement—crossing town feels like the other end of the world and not something most people are eager to do two days in a row.

My immediate reaction was, "Holy shit, he said yes to meeting up! Whatever works for him, I am in!" I felt like I *should* say yes, because I was shocked and honored that he even wanted to make time to meet up with me. I was about to hit Send on accepting his suggestion when I got poked by an inside voice saying, "Is this really ideal for you, Tricia? What if you just asked him if he was available Thursday instead or could meet somewhere more central on Wednesday?" It was such a small thing to do, just to ask, and yet I was really struggling with whether to ask or to just gratefully accept his suggested plan. I had put him on a pedestal and felt like I didn't have the right to ask him about an alternative day or place.

I felt like because of what he had accomplished in his life, his time was more valuable. He was more valuable. That I wasn't important enough or valuable enough to ask this gorgeous, successful human if he would even consider another day or place. I mean, he was willing to carve out time in his week for me. How could I go back and even dare to suggest to him a change to his offering and schedule? I knew that I wanted to ask him about other meet-up possibilities, but I was afraid of being rejected. I was afraid of coming off as pushy or ungrateful. I was afraid that I would be kicked out of his contact list by not just saying *yes* to what he suggested. To be clear it wasn't that I really thought he would be difficult, it was that I saw him having more worth than me, so how dare I offer an alternate plan.

By naming all of these fears and doubts, I saw that this was really a self-worth struggle. *Ugh.*

I reminded myself that I am allowed to ask. I am allowed to see that my time is also valuable. I am allowed to put myself out there. I am allowed to believe I am worthy of his time. So, I sent the e-mail asking if he was available Thursday instead, and he said *yes*. It was no big deal!

Where can you start to flex your self-worth muscle more? It doesn't mean that you are putting yourself above others. It is allowing yourself to have a choice, a voice, an opinion, to nurture yourself and listen to yourself just as you would to the person you look up to and admire.

YOUR WORTH ISN'T MALLEABLE

It may sound like such a small thing, sending this friend an e-mail to inquire about meeting on a different day than he suggested, but it was huge to me to face my own self-worth struggle and to remind myself that my worth was not malleable depending on who I was relating to.

I think that is a common thing that we do. We expand and contract our worth depending on who we are in the company of. For example, if it was one of my old college or touring friends, I wouldn't have hesitated about suggesting we meet on a day that was more accommodating to me. But if it was someone who had fame, like an artist I had worked with, even if I knew they were not busy at all and not working on anything, would I have hesitated like I did with this person?

Think about it: Who do you minimize your worth around? Where do you allow your self-worth to be malleable?

You Are Enough.

You Are Enough.

You Are So Enough.

Right Now—As You Are.

No Matter Whose Company You Are In.

Do you believe it? If not, what doubt, fear, worry, or judgment is not letting you believe it? What *should* is holding you back?

And—heads up!—once you face this head on, it likely won't be overcome forever. These "enough" battles will continue to surface—perhaps every single day for the rest of your life (hey, just being real with you). We have been set up to look outside of ourselves to be validated, and while external validation is not bad, you can't run on it alone. The most important thing is for you to validate you. It is a daily, moment-to-moment, inside job. Because if you aren't claiming it for yourself, you really will never fully be able to accept it from others.

When talking to Talia Pollock, the hilarious author of *Party in Your Plants*, for my *Claim It!* podcast, she brought

"The most important thing is for you to validate you. It is a daily, moment-to-moment, inside job. Because if you aren't claiming it for yourself, you really will never fully be able to accept it from others."

up something I really hadn't given much thought to but that I overwhelmingly agreed with. For those of us who have noticed how our bodies react to certain foods and so therefore choose not to eat them, it actually takes daily boldness to suggest eating at restaurants that don't make us sick, to ask about ingredients, to double-check with a server that a bun is in fact gluten-free because it looks too good to be true. It seems laughable, but I have most definitely gotten eye rolls from people I was dining with for politely asking for a modification so that I didn't eat something that would make me sick for weeks. And I still have to fight with myself to speak up and check!

It can be a real struggle to nicely ask about ingredients and to overcome feeling like I am a burden or high maintenance in order to not feel miserable from eating something that my body doesn't agree with. I actually know people who will just eat the thing that makes them feel sick when they are in social situations because they would rather deal with the physical struggle afterward than the emotional self-worth struggle of asking for something else or modifying what is offered for fear of offending others or appearing difficult.

Where may you be sacrificing your health, your peace, your time, because deep down you are struggling with your own enough-ness? Because you feel that you *should* be easygoing, you *should* do what everyone else wants, you *should* be honored that they said yes to your invitation, you *should* say yes?

Are there people in your life who you slink back, shrink yourself, become more of a yes person around, because of who they are, how they are, or what they have accomplished? I am not saying to not respect people or to not be adaptable. I would have totally been cool if he wasn't able to meet on Thursday. The issue is that I wasn't even going to put myself out there, to ask—when I knew that what I was about to say yes to wasn't ideal for me.

You could think I was just being a generous person and making his life easier by going along with his plan. How nice, considerate, and easygoing of me. Just like when we say, "Oh, I don't care where we eat. You choose." While that may be the truth, there may be a little self-worth struggle happening. How dare you choose where to eat? I mean, if you were on your own, what options would you be choosing from? What keeps you from voicing those choices?

The next time you are asked to choose the plans, movie, meal, etc. and you would usually reply with, "I don't care—you choose," look a little deeper. Do you really, totally not care? Do you not have any preferences at all? Why aren't you allowing yourself to have an opinion? Why are you hesitating to make a suggestion? Sometimes you really may have zero interest in making the choice—awesome. Just make sure the reason you aren't speaking up isn't from fear of being rejected, judged, or being thought of as difficult.

You are worthy of picking the movie, day, time, plans, restaurant. Obviously, we won't always get our choice. We will need to compromise, take turns, make suggestions, get feedback, but **please allow yourself to be worthy of having an opinion. Please allow yourself to be worthy of having a choice. Please allow yourself to be worthy of being heard, seen, accepted**. Notice where you may be sacrificing your own joy, pleasure, time, even health because you want to make it easy for others. Notice where you ignore your own needs because you want to come off as likeable and easygoing. Notice where you may be putting their worth over your own.

> Please allow yourself to be worthy of being heard, seen, **accepted**.

Notice where you are questioning your *enough-ness*. And keep reminding yourself that:

You Are Enough.

You Are Enough.

You Are So Enough.

Right Now—As You Are.

No Matter Whose Company You Are In.

CHAPTER 9

BUT I REALLY DON'T WANT TO . . .

At this point in the book, I hope that you are starting to notice the *shoulds* and to explore and choose your own **wants**. You may be really pumped about living a life of **wants** and have fully committed to F'ing the *Shoulds*, but you also still may be doubting that living a life of pure **wants** is possible. Like it sounds good in theory, but what about all of those tasks and to-dos like cleaning, returning e-mails, running errands, and more? Most of these things can show up as a *should* and are very low on the **want** scale (at least for me). What about those *shoulds* that feel like they *should* be **wants**? Like when we're asked to help our friends, or volunteering. We can't go through life as selfish assholes, only prioritizing our own **wants**.

Have no fear, I am here to prove to you that you actually can live a life of only choosing your **wants** and not living in the *shoulds*—even for those things you might *not* think that you **want** to do. It just takes awareness, mindfulness, and some perspective shifting to ask yourself a few questions. You may actually transform your *should* into a true **want**.

I WANT TO DO THE DISHES!

I remember the first time this *should/want* struggle came up for me. It was that first summer, when I initially committed to a life of *no shoulds*. I began to feel that nagging *should* feeling inside. I *should* do the dishes. Oh crap, no *shoulds*! But I don't really **want** to do the dishes. I mean, does anyone really ever **want** to do the dishes—maybe only when it means they are escaping another task? I'm not going to lie, sometimes I choose doing the dinner dishes over playing dolls with my daughters for the zillionth time a day. Sorry, girls, momma is doing the dishes now. But generally, *no*, doing the dishes or any type of cleaning does not ever initially show up as a **want** for me. It is simply a necessity. The dishes have to be cleaned so that I can then use them again (and not be living in a constant mess).

I was so committed to eliminating *shoulds* from my life that I couldn't force myself to do the dishes because I *should*, or even because I needed to, because that still left a heavy, unmotivating energy on me. But to just swap out the word *should* for **want** and to tell myself that I **wanted** to do the dishes felt like a lie, because it was. *Until* I was able to shift it from a *should* to a **want** by asking myself a few questions to look deeper at the task or *should* at hand.

This dilemma created a simple exploration of weighing out my feelings of obligation. I asked myself:

Why do I feel I *should* do the dishes?

Why would I want to do the dishes?

How will I feel after I do the dishes?

I had to look beyond the immediate task that was weighing on me to see why I would **want** to do this, what the end result would be, and how that end result would make me feel. As that was what I really wanted: **the end result.**

When the dishes are done, I can then use them again when I need them. The kitchen is neat, clean, and organized. When the kitchen is neat and clean, I feel free, clear, and like a weight has been lifted. I love having a clean kitchen, with everything in its place. So, look at that, *I do want to do the dishes*! By looking at the end result that I **want**, I approach the task by choice, without feeling like a heavy *should* blanket is weighing me down because I really **want** to be doing something else.

By examining the *should*, you can turn it into a want, which will quickly steer you out of procrastination and into action. It will keep you connected to *why* you are doing what you are doing so that you don't feel resentful or burdened. By examining the *should* and not feeling like a prisoner to it, you will get to see *what* is motivating that nagging feeling and become empowered to get into action by claiming your ***want***.

Still to this day, I sometimes see the counter or sink filled with dishes and feel the weight that I *should* do them. Each time, I see that as an opportunity to examine the feeling and my priorities. Some days, I choose not to do them, and I don't feel bad about that choice or feel the weight of *should* looming on me. I weigh out my choices and can see, yeah, the dishes need to be done, but right now I **want** to go to sleep, or I **want** to get out the door without feeling rushed, or I **want** to play with my kids. So I actively choose not to do the dishes right now and to get to them later. And when I get to them later, if the "I *should* have already done these" feeling comes up, I steer myself out of feeling ashamed, beating myself up, and calling myself lazy by reminding myself of the choice I made. I remind myself *why* I prioritized what I did, and then I turn on some good music, a podcast, or a show and choose to do those fucking dishes with ease and maybe even a little fun.

> By examining the *should*, you can turn it into a **want**, which will quickly steer you out of procrastination and into action. By examining the *should* and not feeling like a prisoner to it, you will get to see *what* is motivating that nagging feeling and become empowered to get into action by claiming your **want**.

HOW WILL IT FEEL?

Another *should* that can show up for me is around moving my body. I suffer from chronic pain and other issues that come along with fibromyalgia. I often feel best lying down, which can make it highly unmotivating to get up and get in some physical movement. Yet I know from experience that movement actually does help how I feel. When I feel like I *should* exercise, and it's not easy to swap out *should* with **want**, I again get to ask myself some questions:

Why do I feel I *should* do it?

Why would I *want* to do it?

How will I feel when I do it/after I do it?

I **want** to move my body because I always feel better after I do. After I exercise, the tightness I feel melts away. I feel centered, alive, at ease, and like I can take on the world. When I am feeling like crap and my body is not up to the movement, I remind myself that I have felt like this before and how movement helped me. I play the tape through to the end, and that gets me to try it, to choose it, and ultimately, to **want** it instead of *shoulding* on myself.

And like the dishes, sometimes I can also see that right now, I am not feeling it. I don't feel like I have the energy, and rest feels more important. So I ask myself, "What can I do to get even a glimpse of those feelings that movement gives me?" I could journal, read a good book to allow myself to tune out and rest, I could call a friend, or do some stretching right in bed. This questioning allows us to have choices. Even though, yes, I can see that having a clean kitchen is ideal and that exercise helps to calm my mind and energize the body, it doesn't mean I always have to choose them.

Let's say that you **want** to feel better in your body, so you **want** to eat nutrient-dense foods. But maybe you also **want** a delicious cookie or a slice (or whole) pizza or to enjoy a beer. Those choices are allowed because you get to choose! The shame, guilt, and weight you feel from eating those things when feeling like you *should* have chosen something "better" are (in my opinion) way more toxic than eating the cookie or pizza or drinking the beer and allowing yourself to enjoy what it is you **wanted**.

By not always falling victim to your *shoulds*, you give yourself the freedom of choice. You give yourself permission to choose *and* to not shame yourself for your choice. You are empowering yourself to listen and nurture yourself all day long, each and every day.

> By not always falling victim to your *shoulds*, you give yourself the freedom of choice. You are empowering yourself to listen and nurture yourself all day long, each and every day.

SHOWING UP WITHOUT THE *SHOULD*

Now let's talk about acts of service. You know, volunteering to help out friends and loved ones, offering to bake cookies for the school bake sale, being the room mom, even things like going to a funeral. Those things that are good things but may actually show up more as *shoulds* than **wants**.

Be honest with yourself, it's okay. You are not a bad person if you sometimes do things for others out of what feels like karmic obligation. Some acts of service may be an easy, heart open, 1,000 percent immediate *yes* for you, while others may feel a bit more like a heavier *should*.

Of course, you likely do **want** to offer your support, but you also have all of these other things you **want** to do and a full schedule of demands on your regular life that leave you not fully able to show up, support, and contribute all the time. Or maybe what you **want** is to not be doing anything and to be in your PJs on your couch all day. You may have said yes with clear supportive intentions, but as the date nears, you find yourself becoming resentful that you said yes and have to take time, money, etc. to do this thing and be of service. You **want** to be a generous, giving person, but you also have your own shit to handle and your own self to take care of, first and foremost.

Instead of committing and/or showing up out of *should* obligations, allow yourself the opportunity to understand your choice to support and be of service. Ask yourself:

Why do you *want* to show up?

Why did you or do you *want* to say yes?

How does it feel to do things for others?

How does it feel when others do things for you?

Did you say yes to being the room mom simply because you felt you *should*? Were you buying into the BS that in order to be a good mom you have to be a room mom? Did you sign up for it because Anna's mom did, and she always acts like she is the better mom, and you feel like she is always judging you? Or did you say yes because you truly want to be a part of your child's school experience in that way?

When you feel inclined to say yes to something *and*:

- It starts to feel more like an obligation that is weighing on you.

- You hear that little (or loud) voice inside saying, "I wish I could just stay home today, work on my project, do _____," instead of "I **want** to do (insert act of service here)."

- You are gritting your teeth instead of truly feeling called to give your time, attention, and money to be of service and show up for others.

Stop and ask yourself, Why do I want to do this?

Of course, you do **want** to be the good friend, the generous person, the giver, and the do-gooder, the person who shows up. But when you start to feel the weight of the *should*, or wishing you had more time for you instead of having to do this thing you said yes to—go deeper. Consider *how it will feel* to show up, do the thing, be of service, and do it from a true and real place, because you do **want** to. *Or* allow yourself to say no!

Don't show up just because you said yes, because you want others to see you being generous, because it is what is expected of you as a good person, because they do so much for you, so you feel obligated to be there for them. Do it because you truly **want** to. Turn (or return) your motivation into a true and real **want**. And imagine how much different it will feel coming from that place to you and to them. It feels clean and clear. You will feel present, grounded, and alive. You will feel your heart guiding you instead of your resentment, worries of what others will think of you, or some tally-keeping comparisons.

And then, likewise, you will also feel clear and aligned when you do find that you **want** to say no. You can say no without feeling selfish, without feeling shame, without making yourself feel like a bad person. You can create boundaries around your time, money, and energy. And doing so will make the times when you do show up, volunteer, and say yes that much more important and valuable.

When you say yes, you will be showing up because you **want** to. And that will be felt by you *and* by them.

MAKE IT FUN

Another one of my favorite hot tips to turn your *shoulds* into **wants** is to make it fun!

Sometimes a *should* comes up, and even after asking yourself the questions of *why* and *how*, you are still not really feeling that **want** energy. But some things are unavoidable; they have to get done. That's when I ask myself:

How can I approach this with fun, freedom, and ease?

For example, I personally am not a fan of running errands. I buy most things online and use services like Instacart when it makes sense, *but* for the times the errands really do need to be done, I ask myself, "How can I make this fun? What can I do to feel free and at ease?"

For me that looks like wearing headphones as I shop and listening to a podcast or music that lights me up. Sometimes I even bribe myself with a fun drink or treat. Yes, I am a grown-ass adult, and I bribe myself. Say what you will, but it works! I also sometimes bribe myself to **want** to exercise by putting a TV show on in the background. I make it fun, and I make it work for me! You can turn your *shoulds* into **wants** by approaching them with a feeling of freedom and fun instead of feeling like you have been taken hostage by your tasks and to-dos.

MY NOT-SO-SECRET SUPERPOWER

While catching up with a fellow momma, entrepreneur, and best-selling author whom I look up to, I was surprised when *she* asked *me*, "Tricia, I don't get it. How are you doing so much with no help? Your partner is on tour, you have no childcare, you have two toddlers at home, you live with fibromyalgia, and yet you are consistently putting out content and taking care of yourself and your family. How did you read a full novel this week, ride your Peloton bike multiple times, wake up before your kids for morning yoga, put out a podcast and a video, make all of those social posts, run your program, and share about my program all while only working minimal hours and prioritizing your health? Seriously, what is your secret?"

It's actually very simple. I live from a place of **want**, not *should*.

That is it! Every. Single. Day. This little mind trick is what keeps me showing up for my life, for my dreams, for my now! I don't have any magical get-shit-done superpowers. I don't wake up motivated and leaping for joy at all the big and small things that I get to do that day. I am not an overachiever. And I am in no way at all type A. *This* is my superpower. Seeing the *shoulds* under the surface, excavating them, and getting real with each one to see *why* I **want** to do the things that are so freaking easy to just keep putting off and allowing myself to dismiss the things that I really don't need or want to do.

That's how I am consistently showing up, putting myself out there, putting my ideas and dreams into action, and fully living my life while actually enjoying it and not burning out. And yes, while I am a magical, powerful badass, *so are you*! F-ing the *shoulds* and choosing my **wants** is my superpower, and it can be yours too.

I am telling you—you *can* live a life of **wants**. Of your **wants**. And it is for everyone's benefit, as it makes you completely aligned, intentional, and clear on what you are doing and why you are doing it. Plus, there is the added bonus of calling out your own procrastination so that you are truly showing up for yourself and the life that you tell yourself that you **want**. I dare you to try it right now! What is something you are procrastinating on? Ask yourself:

Why would I want to do it?

How will I feel once I do it?

How can I approach this with fun, freedom, and ease?

And then jump in. You got this.

CHAPTER 10

I WANT TO— BUT I DON'T HAVE TIME (AND OTHER EXCUSES).

All right, I know that we both know that there is a difference in **wanting** to do something and actually doing it. And so it doesn't mean that by simply changing your word choice and getting clear on your **wants** that you will actually do all the things. I too can suffer from nonaction and not doing the things that I do **want** to do.

After having kids and losing my precious me time, I longed to wake up early to do yoga, drink a cup of hot coffee in silence, journal—to exist without being constantly needed. It was clear to me that if I really **wanted** those things, my only choice was to wake up before my kids in order to give myself that time. My kids woke up *so* early though! Which meant I would need to wake up even earlier to get a sliver of time for myself. I love to sleep. I love a warm, cozy bed. As I mentioned, I suffer from chronic pain, so getting out of my cozy bed in the morning is a real challenge for me. Waking up earlier than my early-rising kids was much easier said than done. But I was so clear that I did **want** to wake up early, and I could see that it was for my overall best to do so. So why wasn't I just magically flying out of my bed before dawn?

Even though I was telling myself that I **wanted** to wake up early and could easily name all the reasons why, I struggled for months to pull myself out of bed. I set my alarm at all different times. I slept in my yoga leggings. I tried different songs as an alarm with hopes that they would motivate or dance me out of bed. Nothing was getting me out of my bed, except my kids. One week, I even settled on "bed yoga." If I stay in bed and do some stretches, that's the same thing, right?

What finally got me out of bed before the sun came up and got me to truly commit and start waking up early was, instead of telling myself that it was so hard or telling myself that I was trying, I started to tell myself that I *am* someone who wakes up early to do yoga. That *is* who I am. I envisioned myself being that person. And while that is still "easier said than done," it anchored me in a new way that truly made me **want** to show up for myself, my **want**, and the version of myself that I envisioned.

Once the mental anchor was in, I still needed the physical anchor. I needed to feel it in my body. I needed to feel how it felt to do the thing that I **wanted** to do. For me, reminding myself of how good it feels to do the thing—whether it be body-opening yoga, sending the e-mails that I have been putting off, or having the challenging conversation—is a big pull to get me into action. For this, though, I didn't have a memory to pull on, as I had yet to wake up before the sun came up to do yoga. So I had to just start somewhere. Instead of feeling like, "Damn, there goes another early morning. I missed my chance," when my kids pulled me out of bed, I would do yoga then. I'd do *any* minutes of it with my kids climbing on me or get them breakfast and then do a few minutes. Even though I wasn't meeting my vision, by starting somewhere, I was able to get a bigger glimpse at how it would feel to fully step into the vision I had created and **wanted.**

I also started to ask myself to visualize and embody how would it feel to wake up and open up my body and have that time for just me. How would it feel to start the day moving my body? How would it feel to not be woken up by a toddler and then go zooming through my day without the space to pause and slow down to connect to myself? By imagining and drawing myself into this vision, along with telling myself that "I am someone who wakes up early to move my body," I finally did drag myself out of bed one morning and try it. And that is a part of it too. Honestly, sometimes you just have to force yourself to do the damn thing, and then, as soon as you are in it, you *feel* better, and it becomes easier to keep going and keep showing up in the future.

What keeps me showing up for this **want** is feeling the real benefits and impact it makes on my days. Most weeks, I don't do it every day. But what keeps me returning to it time after time is reminding myself of how I feel when I pull my ass out of bed and do the things that make me feel good versus when I stay in the cozy bed until my kids drag me out. Oh right, I do **want** to get out of bed and have that sacred me time that leaves me feeling limber, alive, patient, and energized in body and mind all at the same time. And all of these results that I feel do not just impact me, they make me a more grounded and more present mother, friend, business owner, and human.

Which is why I feel that:

1. Self-care can be a real pain in the ass, but it is always worth it.
2. Self-care is the least selfish thing you can do, as the benefits don't just affect you but everyone you come in contact with.

> Sometimes you just have to force yourself to do the damn thing, and then, as soon as you are in it, you *feel* better, and it becomes easier to keep going and keep showing up.

YOU HAVE TIME FOR WHAT YOU MAKE TIME FOR

The fear of being selfish, putting yourself and your needs and **wants** first, can be a real excuse as to why you aren't doing the things you **want**. It is really easy to tell yourself that you don't have time for what you **want** when you are always minimizing your own desires and putting other people's needs first. You may not even realize that you do this. I get it. You have work, school, family, friends—all the life stuff that takes up your time. It may even be things that you love doing and people you love supporting and spending time with. That is great! But if you really, truly do **want** the things that you **want**, the things that you say, "One day, I will do," the things that you say, "If I had *xyz*, I would do," you have to start making time for it, time for you! You have time for what you make time for.

"It is really easy to tell yourself that you don't have time for what you *want* when you are always minimizing your own desires and putting other people's needs first."

You have to start somewhere. You have to make some space. You have to start claiming any amount of time for what you **want**.

ANY MINUTES IS MORE THAN NO MINUTES

A huge everyday motivator for me that gets me out of bed to do the yoga and to just start, to just do, to get into it and do all of the other things that I **want** to do but say I don't have time for or will do later, is telling myself, "Any minutes is more than no minutes."

When I first imagined this early-morning yoga, I told myself I would do 45 minutes, then I told myself 30, then I just started to tell myself that any minutes is more than no minutes. I realized the amount of time I was trying to commit to felt daunting or I simply just didn't have it, as my kids started waking up even earlier! And by having a very low bar, almost no bar, it allowed me to get the F up and do any minutes.

I was living into the story that if I didn't do at least 45 minutes of yoga, it was like I didn't even do any, which was a full-blown *should* and a way to keep myself in not enough-ness. Like, oh you did yoga, but only five minutes. That isn't enough. You *should* be doing more, if you are a real yogi. Okay, inner voice, like what do you even mean by being a real yogi? What is it that I am **wanting** to get out of yoga? How it makes me feel in my body and my mind. If I can feel *any* better in a few minutes—isn't that better than not doing any because I don't have time (or just won't commit) for a full 45 minutes? I mean, I likely will never get on my mat again if I tell myself I have to do at least 45 minutes. It's easy for me to do that in an in-person class, but at home it literally feels impossible to me. And what an asshole move that, instead of celebrating the fact that I did any, I told myself that I am not enough for not doing more? Geez, the bullshit that consumes our minds and lives. I mean, really, why are we such jerks to ourselves?

So I fully embrace **any minutes**, and some days I do 30 minutes, and some days I do 5, and I feel good about actually doing *any* minutes because even in those 5, I do feel the difference.

Soon, I was applying this phrase/idea to everything. As you heard in the previous chapter, I don't love to do dishes, or really any type of cleaning. Vacuuming is the only cleaning task that I can really get down with, but it's still not my first choice of things to do with my time. But when I tell myself that any minutes is more than no minutes, I get shit done! Or I tell myself this other favorite, "Just five minutes," because it is really hard to argue that I don't have time, patience, or energy for just five minutes.

I apply this any minutes and/or just five minutes to pretty much everything in my life, and because of it I am consistently showing up and doing all the things. The things that I put off because they feel scary or too big or too hard. The annoying things that I wish I could just pay someone else to do but can't afford to. The things that I **want** to do but don't have a clue as to where to start so I keep putting them off and never start. The things I try to tell myself that I don't have time for—all of it. And **over and over again I prove to myself that baby steps are steps.**

When you keep making those itty-bitty steps, you actually do make shit, and shift happens. By focusing on doing just a little, you end up making a huge impact that otherwise you may never have even made a dent in because you were telling yourself that you don't have time, you don't know how, it's too hard, and other excuses. Instead of living into *shoulds* and the idea of how you think or have been programmed to believe you *should* do things, feel about things, and more, you will actually consistently show up for yourself and your **wants**.

> Baby steps are steps. When you keep making those itty-bitty steps, you actually do make shit, and shift happens.

Any minutes *is* more than no minutes. Once I started to use this for the little stuff and the big stuff, I realized that I wasn't making moves toward some of my big **wants** because I didn't have time for the vastness of them. So I just kept putting these dreams and ideas out in the vast someday, or next month, next year. *Or* I wouldn't even allow myself to see my **wants** as real possibilities, because I mean, how the heck would I do them? Not just with the amount of time I had, but also with my resources, experience, and more. It sucks how often it is easier for us to make up excuses and tell ourselves no instead of believing what could be possible and actually trying. It is so easy to put things off and say you don't have time, but it is also pretty damn easy to commit to just five minutes! And then another five, and another five, and another five. We can break down gigantic ideas into little baby steps and tackle them day by day.

> It is so easy to put things off and say you don't have time, but it is also pretty damn easy to commit to just five minutes.

Honestly, a lot of the **wants** that we put off can show up for us as *shoulds* because they feel hard, annoying, and scary. And oftentimes these things will only take 2–15 minutes to do, and when they are done, it will be like a massive weight has been lifted, and you will feel like a fucking boss at life. Try it out, will you? **You can commit to just a few minutes!**

MY PROCRASTINATION BUSTER

My any-minutes and only-five-minutes mantras are major procrastination busters for me. Yet sometimes I still find myself stalling, distracting myself, doing all the other things besides that thing I so **want** to do—like write this book. Yep, while writing the book *F the Shoulds*, I was definitely F'ing my *shoulds* daily, ha!

So what do I do to get myself out of the procrastination cycle and get the motivation to dive headfirst into what is showing up as a big, scary, giant undertaking, like writing this book? Because of course, while I distract myself by doing all the other things, I can feel an invisible, heavy *should* tapping on my shoulder, telling me, "You *should* be doing that thing you **want** to do!" Ugh, those nagging *shoulds*! They even *should* at me to show up for my **wants**! And while the *shoulds* are relentless and so freaking annoying, I now use each *should* that comes my way as an opportunity to look within and call myself and the world out on its bullshit.

The trick that has me showing up day after day to write and write and edit and edit this book, along with my any-minutes trick, is my *why*. When I hear that nagging *should*, I get to ask myself over and over, "Tricia, *why* do you **want** to open that file on your computer and start typing? Why do you **want** to read this document for the bazillionth time looking for ways to improve it even though it feels daunting?" **I allow my *why* to motivate my *want*, which gets me to do the doing.** Getting clear on my *why* helps me move past the fears, doubts, worries, comparisons, and feelings of not enough-ness that try to stop me from doing what deep down I know I **want** to do.

> I allow my **why** to motivate my **want**, which gets me to do the doing.

While the doing can sometimes feel like an impossible task, once I am in it—once I am in the doing—I always feel aligned, alive, and like a badass for taking charge of my life. Whether that is by doing the dishes, getting on my spin bike, or typing into this document that *will* turn into something you are reading in your home, years later.

Allow your why to call you into the doing!
Why do you *want* to do it?
And also imagine *how* awesome you will feel once you do it.

PRIORITIZE YOUR PRIORITIES

Often during my kids' afternoon rest time, I can feel over-whelmed with how I want to use my time. There are so many things that I **want** to do! I **want** to exercise. I **want** to just chill out and rest. I **want** to get work done. I **want** to call a friend and connect with them without small people vying for my attention. They are all **wants**, so which **want** ~~should~~ *do* I do?

How I sort through my **wants** to prioritize my priori-ties is to weigh them out and feel them out. I also remind myself that I don't have to just choose one; I can delegate a chunk of time for each! I check in to acknowledge each **want** and the *why* that motivates it and see which feels like the priority. Which **want** feels like the most fulfilling first choice right now? It varies on different days! Sometimes I **want** movement first. Sometimes I **want** to get the work out of the way. Sometimes I **want** to just lie down and rest first. And then I give myself blocks of time and allow myself to be in each **want** during that time. Often that looks like 30 minutes of resting (lying in bed with a novel or memoir), then 30 minutes of exercise to wake up my body and mind, then the last hour for work! Sometimes I **want** movement *and* I have a deadline to meet for work. So I choose 15 min-utes of movement and then dive into the work that I will feel so good about having done on deadline!

Allow yourself to actually get in tune with *your* pri-orities and how it will make you feel by doing them. Don't get distracted by what you have taken on to believe you *should* be doing with your time and what you *should* be prioritizing or by what you prioritized yesterday or last week or whenever. **Allow yourself to come at it in the present**

moment each time so that you can really be clear with yourself about what you are doing and why.

As I said before, you have time for what you make time for. Nobody else is going to give you time to make it happen. The world isn't going to come to a stop for you. Prioritize your priorities and be clear with yourself that *you* are your own priority! And if you get stuck in decision fatigue, unable to make a choice, make *any* choice! You are always allowed to choose again if it ends up not being what you **want**. That's called living and learning. It's a necessary ingredient to life.

MAKE YOUR WANT WORK FOR YOU

Another reason I find myself *not* doing **wants** is because the way I see other people doing them doesn't fit for me. Like meal prep, for example. Of course I **want** to meal prep, because I really love having food ready to heat up and eat. I often end up with no breakfast and a shitty lunch if I don't have anything prepped or any leftovers to heat up. But the way that meal prepping was displayed to me looked like so much work! You have to take an entire day (Sunday, they usually say) to go grocery shopping and then cook for hours? Yeah, doing that with two toddlers felt impossible and stressful and just not what I **wanted** to do with my Sunday, even if I did **want** the end result. But I really, really, really **wanted** to have prepped meals!

So I decided to fuck the methods I was being sold and do it in a way that worked for me! What that looked like was simply cooking extra on the days that I cooked. Say Monday I was motivated to make a big batch of soup, then throw rice in a rice cooker *and* roast a ton of veggies. Bam,

"The world isn't going to come to a stop for you. Prioritize your priorities and be clear with yourself that *you* are your own priority! You are always allowed to choose again if it ends up not being what you *want*."

I cooked food I could easily reheat for a couple of lunches while making dinner. Easy peasy! That is my version of meal prepping, and it works for me! You get to choose what works for you. You get to make your **want** work for you today, next week, next year, and ongoing. Your **wants** will shift, and what works for you will shift. One day, all-day Sunday meal prep may be my thing!

Recently, I started craving green juice. I used to make it daily; I even toured with a juicer. But again, with kids and a change in life, it no longer felt easy. For months I said I wanted to juice. I would buy the produce and not actually juice it. I realized I needed to make it easier for myself—not harder—so I started buying giant premade green juices from Costco. I knew it wasn't as fresh as what I would make at home, but it was better than nothing! And again, once I tasted it and had some in my body, it reminded me of how good it felt. Which motivated me to start buying the produce to juice or blend at home—when it felt easy for me. Sometimes I buy the giant premade jug. Sometimes I buy the ingredients and juice at home.

The lesson here is, **stop making it so hard for yourself to do your wants!** Stop being a perfectionist about it. Stop *shoulding* on yourself and judging yourself for what works for you in order to get started and keep going. Make your **wants** work for you.

DO YOU WANT TO, OR DO YOU FEEL THAT YOU *SHOULD* WANT TO?

Have you ever felt inner or outer pressure to do something that is meant to be good for you? Like you feel you *should* **want** to do it—because you know it will be good for you—so you tell yourself you do want to. But you never do it. Meditation is something that haunts me like this. It's everywhere! Everyone is telling me about their meditation practice and asking me about mine. And honestly, while yes, I understand the benefits of it, I am still so resistant to it! Because to me it shows up as more of a *should* than a true **want**, like I *should* **want** to do it. Do I really **want** to meditate? Yes! No! I don't even know anymore! Okay, why would I **want** to meditate? It has the potential to make me feel calm and centered. People *always* say how transformational and supportive it is. I love that feeling of post-yoga bliss, lying in Savasana, and I imagine it has a similar feeling.

Do I actually **want** to try it and I just haven't committed to making it happen? Or am I feeling I *should* meditate because I hear everyone else talk about how it helps them, so I feel I *should* **want** to do it? Is it tied to a fear of being judged for not doing it? Or a not enough-ness or comparison story? Do I feel I *should* **want** to because that is what all "good" motivational people do?

By feeling out the *should* energy that comes my way as an opportunity to ask myself questions, I get to uncover what it is underneath the surface that is motivating me and to clarify if it is really a *should* or a **want**. This way I can make the best choice for myself in each instance. Using my example, if you are feeling you *should* meditate and aren't truly able to get yourself to the **want** space— you can ask yourself what else you could do to give you the results you are seeking. Meditation is fabulous, and you and I will likely benefit from it. But forcing or *shoulding* yourself into it isn't fun and may hinder the results you are looking for, as you will be showing up with resistance.

You also get to give yourself permission to see that it is perfectly okay if you decide you don't want to meditate. By exploring the *should*, you give yourself permission to "whatever it is" *your* way. You do **want** the results of meditation but just can't get yourself to sit down and be still? Try a walking meditation, a dancing meditation, a guided visualization meditation, a mantra meditation; meditate to music that moves you. My friend, author and health coach Robyn Youkilis, busted a big meditation *should* myth for me and many others when she started offering guided meditations on social media using Phish and electronic dance music. She would also share meditations when lying in bed, in an Uber, on the subway, and in more ways and places that we are wired to think aren't for meditating. The reason I had been so resistant to meditation is because I was only seeing it as a sitting-in-an-uncomfortable-position-in-silence *should*. Robyn makes it appealing, fun, and diverse, and I freaking love that!

Make it work for you. Make it easy (or easier) for you. Make it fun for you. See that it doesn't have to be 20 minutes of sitting in an uncomfortable position, not allowing any thoughts to come into your mind, and getting upset with yourself when you fail. You get to choose. You get to try things on and out.

So often we see things as one way. The way we were initially introduced to something. The way we have been taught we *should* do it. The way that we see others doing it. We forget that we have the freedom to make it our own. To make it be joyful, to make it easy.

Allow yourself the freedom to break out of the box you were sold and make it work for you instead of working against you.

CHAPTER 11

WHAT ARE YOU REALLY SAYING?

Okay, we are 11 chapters in. Are you starting to notice the energy of things that show up as *shoulds* and how swapping out the actual word itself can change how it lands and how it feels? While the majority of this book is about tackling our own thoughts, feelings, doubts, and all the *shoulds* rooted into us, I couldn't not talk about *shoulding* at and on others. Especially if you are going to follow my lead and kick the word completely out of your life. Have you noticed, like Mona did, how embedded the word is in many people's vernacular (including your own)? Have you been noticing how often this word comes at us and out of us? In conversation with others is a big way that can happen, and I myself discovered that in these cases, **want** wasn't always the ideal word to swap it with.

I want to set you up for total *F the Should*s success! So I feel it is important to explore different possibilities on how to say what it is you are trying to say and be heard without using the damn *S*-word and projecting that energy onto others. I mean, what are you saying or asking, really? That is what eliminating *shoulds* in conversations did for me. It slowed me down and made me get **super clear about what it is that I am really saying, why I am saying it, and how I want it to land for others. The impact of our word choice doesn't just affect us, it affects the people we are talking to.** By taking out the *shoulds*, you will be so much more direct, intentional, and compassionate with your words and the impact they have the potential to make.

Something I noticed is that when I fight to navigate around *shoulds* in conversations with others, it feels like I am doing one of two things. One, making myself smaller, like, "Me? Oh, I don't know. What do *you* think we *should* do?" As if I am not worthy of an opinion or I am afraid of what they will think if I do actually express my opinion or choice. Or two, it can come off as if I am a pushy know-it-all, like I know better than you do: "You *should* wake up early to do yoga. That is what I do." And I know from personal experience that *shoulding* at people can potentially make them stop listening, put up a wall, and turn away from you rather than opening up to listen and receive your loving support, guidance, and advice.

WHY ARE YOU SAYING IT?

Besides monitoring and swapping out the *shoulds*, a good practice is to ask yourself, *What* are you really saying, and *why* are you saying it? This can be an in-the-moment catch before you open your mouth—or you can catch yourself in conversation to bring yourself back to the point. Why am I saying this? Why am I offering my opinion? Why am

I asking them this? Why am I in a conversation with this person, even?

Do you love and respect them and want to show them support? Have you been in a similar experience and feel that you have valuable information to share? Do you feel like you have to have an answer or reply because of the fear of being judged or not enough? Do you want advice? Do you look up to the person? Do you want them to see you a certain way?

Get clear with yourself so that your words have clear intentions and energy behind them. Be confident, clear, and compassionate in your language and conversations, whether you are replying, commenting, sharing, or asking. You can feel the energy of words and what is behind them. Get clear on your *why* to shift your attention, intention, and delivery. Doing this will give you a greater chance of being heard.

SEEKING ADVICE

The *shoulds* can definitely surface when asking for opinions and advice. I *love* to get input, feedback, and advice from people who have been in similar situations and/or have experience with what I am interested in. It won't kill you to ask, "What *should* I do?" But for me, totally eliminating the word had such a big impact on catching my thoughts, beliefs, actions, and more. Catching the word made me slow down and get clear with myself about what I was really thinking or saying. I felt like if I let it slip sometimes, then soon I would get lazier and lazier with my use of it and would then lose all the daily realizations that eliminating the word had given me. *And*, by not using that word, I found replacements that didn't feel so disempowering, like I wasn't handing it all over to someone else. I got to maintain my power, my worth, and my distinction to choose.

Let's look at how taking out *should* gets us clearer on what it is we are really looking for.

Consider how different it would feel to, instead of saying:

What should I do?

to say something like:

If you were in my place,
what would you do and why?

When you were in my position/
just starting out, what did you do?

I would love to hear your feedback/
opinion on this.

What led you to make the choices
that you made?

What do you think about _____?

In these questions you retain your own power and freedom of choice while also giving the person you are talking to reverence and genuinely showing them that you value their feedback and experience. You aren't shrinking. You aren't giving over your choices. You aren't looking for someone else to drive your car for you. **You are stating that you are looking for information but also leaving a lot of space there to remind them and you that you get to take this information from them and still make your own choice.**

Also, they are a reminder to pay attention to *who* you are asking and getting advice from. You can love and respect someone *and* they may not always be the go-to for advice. Like, would you ask someone who is in an unhealthy relationship for advice on your own? Would you ask someone who stays in a job they hate about your career options? Aim to be more discerning with *who* you are asking.

OFFERING ADVICE

I *love* to add my two cents. I love hearing about what people are going through. I am a naturally curious person who loves to ask questions and offer options, ideas, and resolutions. I am a problem solver and a go-getter! *But*, due to my own sensitivity to receiving unwarranted advice and being *shoulded* at—I try really damn hard to do so coming from a space of compassion, love, and respect. Am I sharing this with them because I love them and think they want to know? Am I suggesting this because I have a feeling it will support them? How can I say it with compassion instead of talking at them? How can I make this land so that it doesn't sound like I am telling them what to do or that I know better than them? Do I feel they are even in a space to hear me or want advice?

Consider how different it feels if someone is saying to you:

Have you considered _____?

Or:

Do you want to hear my feedback/opinion? (Wait for a yes.) This is what I would do in your place.

Or:

That sounds (tough/hard/challenging); are you open to my thoughts on it?

Instead of:

You *should* . . .

Think about what you want them to feel, not just what you want them to hear, and that will help you shape your feedback, support, advice, and more.

When sharing something that you love, a way that you have had good results in doing something, or your opinion, try out phrases like:

_____ is what I do/did that works/ed for me.

When I was in a similar position, I did _____.

I recommend _____.

I tried (enter the thing/place/etc.) and loved it. Here is the info if it interests you at all.

If you are making a suggestion, instead of we *should*, try out:

Let's do _____.

If you want, we can _____.

Do you want to _____?

_____ works best for me.
How do you feel? What works best to you?

ASK FOR CONSENT/PERMISSON

Asking feels so much better than *shoulding*! When you find yourself wanting to offer opinions, suggestions, support—first ask if the other person is open to and **wants** your advice or feedback before offering it. This establishes a level of respect, trust, and compassion, and shows them that you are truly listening and wanting to support them.

It also helps me to ground my energy and remind myself that their life is their life. Their choices are their choices, and as much as I feel that I may know better or more, or have experience and advice that can help them, I can't live their life for them. We all have to live and learn to find our own way. Some people may be open to advice and listening and will learn from our experiences. Some people just need to learn it themselves. Some people are just not in a space to take in other people's input, and trying to force it on them may create separation instead of connection.

> Their choices are their choices, and as much as I feel that I may know better or more, or have experience and advice that can help them, I can't live their life for them.

By asking before offering, you are creating a safe space for them to be heard, seen, and to open up to you when they are ready. It may not be right now.

USING "I" LANGUAGE

Something I have learned over the years is that when I talk from my own experiences or share how I feel in "I" language, it allows others to listen and open up in a different way. It lands in a way that they can receive without feeling judged, shamed, or wrong. When I focus on me, rather than saying, "You *should* . . . " or telling them what I think they *should* be doing (even if I'm not using the *S*-word), it tones down the energy and makes a space for the other person and I to be more open and accepted.

Back when I was a touring sound engineer, I was not your typical roadie. I rolled off the tour bus when I woke up and did yoga in the parking lot. I traveled with my own juicer to make green juice. I added green powder to my water bottles. I didn't live on Red Bull, Coke (either kind), or other substances. And I also didn't judge all the guys and girls who did. I didn't look at them and grimace and roll my eyes. I didn't brag or preach about what I did or try to persuade anyone to follow in my footsteps. I did me. I took care of myself and did what worked for me. When people asked me why I had so much energy without drinking caffeine, I told them what I did. I shared with them directly from my personal experience. I told them how it helped me—never turning the focus on them and what they were doing or not doing. When they marveled at how I could flip road cases in the truck without later complaining about my back hurting, I told them how the yoga I did helped me build core strength.

I didn't tell them what they *should* be doing to feel better or how they *should* be more like me or the choices I would make if I were them. When they asked or commented, I would share with them what I did, why I did it, and how it helped me using only "I" language. I didn't tell them to try it or act as if I were better, wiser, or smarter. I was speaking purely from my own experience. And what do you know? Soon many of them started asking me for green juice and telling me that they started doing yoga or asking to do it with me.

When someone is talking at me instead of to me, as much as I want to receive and listen, a part of me shuts down. I naturally go in defense mode, and I know that I am not alone in that. We can't make people listen to us, and also, not everything is for everyone. That goes for you and everyone else, including the people that you love and **want** to protect and see flourish. Be mindful of how and why you are giving advice, offering suggestions, and sharing your opinion—even when they are coming to you asking for it.

Allow other people the same benefit that you **want** for yourself—to collect data and make their own choices. And by using "I" language instead of "you" language, what you are saying may actually land with them even more powerfully.

WHAT DO YOU WANT?

I am not saying the *should*-to-**want** switch won't work in conversations with others; it often will. It just depends on what you are saying or asking. I feel that "What do you **want** to do?" feels more inviting than "What *should* we do?" It feels lighter, freer, and more expansive instead of pressurized. It gives the other person space and empowers them to check in with themselves. It also may greatly shift the perspective of the other person.

That same year I committed to giving up the word *should*, I remember visiting my friend who had just opened her own café. She was working around the clock, as they couldn't afford to have employees yet, and she was just bone-dead tired. When she finally finished her closing tasks, she turned to me and asked, "Where *should* we eat?" And I simply replied, "Where do you **want** (brightly, excitedly enunciating the **want**) to eat?" I didn't explain my *should*/**want** mission of changing the world; I just changed the question with that simple word swap, and she felt it.

She had a sudden burst of energy as her eyes widened with excitement at the fact that—oh, right—she had a choice! Like she forgot she was able to actually ask herself what she **wanted** and then also do what she **wanted**. Sure, we were just talking about what to eat for dinner, but that simple word shift reminded her of the power of her own choice. That you can actually eat what you **want**, consider your own opinion, tastes, urges, instead of cycling through *shoulds* all day.

> **Your one-word swap has the power**
> **to impact not just you, but so many others!**
> **Empower your wants and their wants!**

JUST DROP IT

One easy *should* work-around is just dropping it out of the sentence. I saw someone promoting a sale who wrote, "You *should* get one today." They could just as easily and even more directly say, "Get one today!" While that statement is even more direct, doesn't it feel more spacious and like it is a choice, rather than someone waving their finger at you, telling you what to do?

> Dropping the *shoulds* and getting clearer with your words and intentions makes you more intentional, connected, and compassionate.

Another one I caught online was "If you have PCOS, you *should* look into this." This is another one that, for me, feels better just dropping the *should* and shortening it to "If you have PCOS, look into this." **More direct phrasing can actually come off as less pushy.** Eliminating the *should* makes it appeal to me more as a choice rather than making me feel like if I don't follow the advice, I am wrong. It is straightforward yet somehow less bossy without the *should*.

Dropping the *shoulds* and getting clearer with your words and intentions isn't only for your own good. It isn't selfish! It makes you more intentional, connected, and compassionate out in the world too. What are you really saying? Why are you saying it?

More *should* swap options

- I *should* warn you. / I will warn you. / I am warning you.
- Which way *should* I go? / Which way do I go? / Which way am I going?
- *Should* I do this? / Is it advised to do this? / Is it best to do this?
- You *should* . . . / Have you considered . . .
- That *shouldn't* happen. / That isn't fair/right that that happened.
- We *should* get right back to you. / We will get right back to you.
- You *should* know. / Just so you know.
- This *should* be handled ASAP. / This will be handled ASAP.
- *Should* you have further questions. / If you have further questions.
- You *should* try this. / Try this./I think you would enjoy/benefit from this.
- You *should* . . . /In my opinion it would be beneficial for you if you . . .
- You *should* ask (insert name) /Ask (insert name)

CHAPTER 12

WHAT IS MOTIVATING YOUR CHOICES? BEING IN— AND STAYING IN— INTEGRITY.

Definition of Integrity:
*the quality of being honest and having strong moral
    principles; moral uprightness.*
the state of being whole and undivided.

To be honest with others, you have to be honest with yourself. And getting honest with myself has been the key to my ongoing healing and to me truly living my life.

When I had my major *should* revelation years ago, I started to see how often I was making choices, saying things, doing things, and moving through life based on what had been projected at me as *shoulds* without taking time to look deeper at what I was actually saying, doing, and believing, and why.

Why? is a question that I now ask myself all day long. When I feel the invisible *shoulds*, especially. Those damn *shoulds* are sneaky! They try to find deep hiding spots and love to disguise themselves!

I look at *shoulds* as a flashing red traffic signal— demanding me to be alert. I see it. Then I come to a stop, look around, and ask myself, Why?

Why do I **want** to say yes?

Why do I **want** to exercise?

Why do I think that I am not enough?

Why do I feel this way?

Why is this *should* weighing on me?

By always being clear on what is motivating my choices, I am able to show up for everything from a true place of **want**. It allows me to move out of any place of burden, regret, guilt, comparison, or other feelings that can leave me feeling indecisive or funky. I am able to always be clear and aligned. I show up on purpose, not because I said I would, not because I *should*, not because I am paying someone back, not because it is expected of me, not because I am looking for something in return. Because I **want** to.

And that feels damn good. To be clear, aligned, and present coming from a true place of **want**. I may have to shift myself into it before I show up—but I always do! This makes a difference not just to me and how I show up for and experience life, but also how other people experience me.

WHAT IS MOTIVATING YOU?

We all know that we *should* exercise. We know all of the many ways that moving our bodies, getting our heart rate up, sweating, and simply walking benefit not just our physical body but our emotional wellness as well. Yet even those of us who love to move our bodies and feel those endorphins flowing can get stuck feeling the *shoulds* of exercising some days (or most days) rather than the jumping-up-and-down **wanting** to.

So, when I feel the weight of "I *should* exercise" pressing down on me, I clear it up and ask myself, Why would I **want** to exercise? Why do I **want** to exercise? I **want** to because of how it makes me feel in my body and mind. And when I get clear on that, I also let any restrictions or guidelines or *shoulds* around how I exercise and how long I do it for go.

Are you mindful of what is motivating you to exercise or to feel like you *should* be? I was taught that I *should* exercise so that my body would look a certain way. I wasn't taught or guided to exercise for my physical or mental health and how good it would make me feel in body and mind. I was told to do it so I would be thinner. I was led to believe that I *should* look a certain way and I *should* do certain things to try to fit the image that I was sold, and some of that messaging *still* fucks with me.

That is why I **want** you to start asking yourself *why* all day long. So that you can get clear with yourself, get real with yourself, and start to heal yourself from what you have been conditioned to believe about yourself, your worth, your body, and more.

Ask yourself right now:

Why do you exercise or feel that you *should* if you tend to not? Is it because you feel your worth is in what size you are? Or is it because it makes you feel good inside and out? Do you exercise because you are following a checklist that I *should* move my body three-to-five times a week? Or because it reduces stress, clears your mind, and/or lowers your blood pressure? Do you exercise because you think that once you lose those 10 pounds, then you will be chosen for a promotion, as a romantic partner, will finally feel enough? Or because it empowers you and inspires creativity within you?

When you tap into the *should*, you get the chance to choose movement and you get the opportunity to examine *why* you **want** to exercise. In this process you will have to face yourself and see what really motivates you. Are you pushing yourself and *shoulding* yourself to exercise because you are striving to look a certain way, be or stay a smaller size, see a certain number on the scale because you believe then you will be more accepted, more worthy, more loved? Or are you exercising because it makes you come alive, nurtures your mind, strengthens your body, melts away your stress, empowers you, and soothes the pain in your body?

> Ask yourself why you do the things that you do. What is really motivating you? Is it for your own well-being and desires? Or the desire to please others, fit in, and feel worthy?

Ask yourself why you do the things that you do. What is really motivating you? Is it for your own well-being and desires? Or the desire to please others, fit in, and feel worthy enough? If reasons outside of yourself are motivating you, it will likely never fulfill you or be sustainable. You have to **want** it for you, not for what you **want** others to think of you. And to be clear, I think it is perfectly okay to **want** to be fit, to **want** to lose weight, to **want** to gain endurance and muscle. I just **want** you to be clear with *why* you **want** that and what it will mean for you when/ if you reach your goal. I **want** you to accept that you have just as much worth now as you will then. I **want** you to love and appreciate yourself right now, as you are, just as much as you imagine you will when you reach that goal. I **want** your own love and support to motivate you to get there instead of your not enough-ness and disgust with yourself motivating you, and I hope you **want** that too.

> I **want** you to love and appreciate yourself right now, as you are, just as much as you imagine you will when you reach that goal.

WHAT ARE YOU EXPECTING TO GET?

One day I was losing myself in what I thought was some mindless TV as I relaxed at night. I was watching *Jane the Virgin*, and the main character (Jane) called out one of the other characters for her lack of being a true friend. She said that it was a transactional relationship. That the other person (Petra) only ever did things because of what she wanted to get in return. This made me sit up straight and think hard on it. Wow. Are there any relationships that I am in that are transactional? Where am I showing up in my life just to get something in return?

I know what you may be thinking. A lot in life is actually somewhat transactional, but by looking deeper at my intentions and my why, I started to show up as what felt like to me a much more genuine, whole-hearted human. Of course, my wish is for people to treat me how I treat them, but when I tuned in to this transactional idea, I was able to detach from expectations and make sure that I was truly doing things from a place of pure **want**. Which releases those damn feelings of disappointment I talk about in Chapter 4.

That *Jane the Virgin* episode led me to go on a super deep dive, looking at "Wow, where am I doing things, saying things, showing up a certain way with the hopes of being seen as a good person?" Okay, stick with me. Of course, most of us **want** to be known as a good person. We want to be liked. We want to be loved. We **want** to be accepted. I mean, that is the most basic, yet deepest human desire—to be accepted. But what if by coming at everything with the intention of **wanting** to be seen/known as a good person, we were actually not coming from our heart but from our head and not fully being clean with our intentions?

Sort of like if a tree fell in a forest and no one heard it, did it make a noise? If you did a good deed, sent someone a gift, offered your help, sent them a love note cheering them on—and no one acknowledged you for it—do you still feel great about doing it? Or are you looking for some approval for doing it? You are doing it purely because you **want** to, right? Would you be expecting something in return? Are you expecting a thank you? Are you hoping that they will return the favor? If no one acknowledged that you did the thing, would you still feel as good about doing it?

Are you doing it because you truly **want** to, or is there some "I **want** them to love me, accept me, appreciate me" tied in there that may leave you feeling disappointed or taken advantage of if you don't get the reaction you want out of doing it?

Here is an example. I sometimes send products from my product line to friends and podcast guests as gifts. I send the products because I **want** them to have them, to use them, to enjoy them. *And* if they choose to share it on social media with their followers, that is a major bonus! But before I caught on to the idea of transactional actions, intentions, and relationships, I would regularly be disappointed when I sent out products (sometimes when a person had even asked me for them and told me they would share) and then never even got a thank you once they had arrived. Now every time that I send a gift package—even if the person has said, "I love that and I will totally share it!" I get clear with myself. Am I sending out my products and spending money on shipping plus the item cost because I genuinely **want** them to have it and enjoy it, with no strings attached? Or because I **want** them to share it and hopefully that will lead to me selling some? Yes, both things can be true, but I have to feel just as good about sending it and nothing at all happening (including not even receiving a private thank you from them) in order to feel clean, good, and of integrity when I send it out.

When you say yes to helping a friend move or driving them to the airport, when you bring your sick friend soup, when you promote a friend's business, are you doing it because you truly, fully 1,000 percent **want** to? Are you going to still feel great about doing it, even if they never reciprocate? Even if you don't get the acknowledgment that you seek? It is just a shift in awareness and energy to get clear on the true **want**, without these spider webs attached looking for something in return.

Of course, we want our friendships and relationships to not be one-sided. We **want** for the people in our lives to thank and appreciate us. I am not saying to endlessly give and not receive, but to be clear on your intentions and expectations. You can also be clear to say, "Yes, I will help you this weekend. Do I have your word that you will help me when I am in a similar situation?" Be clear with people so that you can cut out the weird vibes, expectations, and hurt that come from not communicating and the disappointment you may feel if you don't get the reaction that you didn't even know you were hoping for. **And the main person you need to be communicating with is** *you*! And also remember that people are human and they forget. Them not saying thank you or returning the favor may not have anything to do with you or their character. They likely just got distracted by life and truly are grateful for you.

IS IT A REAL WANT, OR IS IT PEOPLE PLEASING?

Now let's have a word about people-pleasing behavior, for all of you who are always saying yes, giving, and showing up for everyone. You are an amazing human; I am sure of this. But I want to make sure that you know that you will be loved *even if* you can't do all the things, for all the people, all the time. One of my dearest friends has been a people pleaser as long as I have known her and now in her forties is beginning to recover. We met at age 18, and while I love her deeply, I don't fully trust her, and that sucks.

You see, since I have seen her for years put everyone else's needs first, self-sacrifice over and over again, struggle with stress-related migraines and sicknesses each year, which is likely connected to her always saying yes to others and being such a wonderful, generous human, it is hard for me to trust her word. Does she want company? Does she like this restaurant? Does she want to keep walking? Am I even one of her best friends? Or is she saying yes because she doesn't know how to (or is afraid to) say no and she doesn't want to disappoint me (and everyone else)?

One week that we had plans, I checked in with her a day before because I knew she had had a super full week and wanted to make sure that she truly had the energy and capacity for our plans. I expressed that I was looking forward to spending time with her, but I would totally understand if she wanted to postpone in order to recover. I was so freaking proud of her that she said that she actually did want to cancel because she just needed time to herself after having a busy week and was so grateful to me for setting the stage for that. Yes! I get happy about people telling me they don't want to spend time with me because they are prioritizing their own needs over mine!

I want people to say *yes* to me because they really **want** to and feel 100 percent aligned with their choice, not because they feel that they *should*, or they owe me, or they are afraid of disappointing me, or they think they will get something from it, even if that is me thinking what a generous person and good friend they are. And I **want** other people to feel that from me. That I am there,

CHAPTER 13

BE A YES TO YOU. (SAYING NO AND CREATING BOUNDARIES.)

What resulted from the year that I gave up my dream job of being a touring sound engineer in order to grieve, heal, and give myself the space to dream up a way to wake people up to truly living and enjoying their lives was the creation of a new position for myself back on tour. By giving up the word *should,* and every day becoming aligned with my **wants**, I created a new landscape for myself to dream beyond what I had previously considered possible. I wanted to wake up the world to actually living their lives, so I started with the world I knew. With the very same Grammy Award–winning artists I had toured with as a sound engineer.

I had spent the bulk of the past decade sharing a stage with artists, musicians, and bands from all walks of life and music genres. I witnessed firsthand how much went into these talented beings living their dreams out in the world.

I saw how complicated and exhausting their lives were when they were pulled in every direction with requests from their labels, management, agents, press, fans, loved ones, and more. By F'ing my own *shoulds* and aligning to my **wants**, I envisioned a role for myself in which I could support these artists in staying healthy in body and mind. To keep them grounded and also empower them to stay in integrity with the version of themselves they wanted to be, so they could fully enjoy their dream lives and not resent them or anyone else who was guiding their careers.

I spent my year "off" doing trainings, educating myself, nurturing myself, and envisioning this dream role on tour as I kept uncovering and pursuing my **wants**, and then I made it happen. I made up a job for myself and then pitched my idea to different artists, production managers, and artist managers, most of whom thought I was out of my mind. I didn't let other people's idea of what type of roles *should* and *should not* exist on tour stop me. I just needed one yes, and I got it. They called me the tour Joyologist (the title stuck). It was epic and also challenging.

I had created a massive position for myself, and I was fully committed to it. I was the grounding and empowering person of the tour, making energizing juices, smoothies, and meals to keep the artist healthy. Leading the tour members through yoga every show day to calm and expand their bodies and minds. Vibing out the dressing rooms to make them more welcoming and nurturing. And the biggest part of the role I created for myself was having the "let's get real" talks with the artists. Lovingly calling them out on their shit, digging into what was driving their mood, reminding them they had choices, and lifting them up when they were not awake to their gifts and purpose. I nudged them past the *shoulds* to get clear on what they really felt, what was working, what wasn't, and how to enjoy the parts of the job they didn't love. So they were actually being present to and enjoying the lives they were living on stage and off. So that they were living their own life of **wants**.

I loved what I had created, but I was burned the F out after my tour as a Joyologist to the stars. As the yearlong tour cycle was reaching its end, I decided that I would run away to India. Not just for a few weeks of exploration as a treat. No, I told myself and anyone listening (and those not), I was going away for the unforeseeable future. I gave away all my belongings, not sure where I would go, be, do next. Even though I loved every moment of the job I had created, I was dead tired and wanted to run away from it all to recover. I craved space to reconnect with myself. Seriously, I spent weeks sorting through my belongings, packing, giving things away, and preparing for my adventure, and my only goals for going to India were to write, do yoga, and learn to run. Oh, and spend time at the beach (which is why I started in Kerala in southern India). Nothing about my trip really had anything to do with India.

I had all of these big good-byes and made a huge deal about going away for at least six months because that was the length of the visa, but I figured I could hop onto another country after that, because I was on a journey! I was starting a new life! The night before I left, a friend asked me what I was most excited about, and without any thought I replied, "To not be near anyone I know." Ha ha ha, wait, what did I just say?

I hadn't really spent any time thinking about that as I prepared for this trip, so it even surprised me that it was what came out of my mouth, but as soon as I said it, I knew it was the truth. What I realized very quickly once I landed in India was that this big journey had little to nothing to do with India and everything to do with running away from my life. A life that I loved. **The reality was that I had given up everything and fled the country because that felt easier than saying *no* to friends and loved one's invitations and requests. The only way I could imagine feeling great about prioritizing myself was by being thousands upon thousands of miles away from anyone that I knew.**

Unconsciously, I was afraid of putting myself, my needs, and my **wants** first, because we are so often taught that it is wrong to do. And with no work or grief to hide behind, what would I say? That I just didn't **want** to? I was a giver! I showed up for people! That is who I am and what I wanted people to know me for. I was afraid to say no because I didn't want to be unsupportive or rude. I didn't want to look like an uncaring, self-centered friend. I didn't want them to think that I didn't love them. I feared that by saying no, they would abandon and reject me, but I was abandoning and rejecting my own real desires, needs, and priorities.

I was so afraid of saying no to others and disappointing them, so instead I was repeatedly saying no to myself. By doing this, I was sending myself the message that my own needs were not as important. I was continuously disappointing myself by not feeling as if I were important enough, valuable enough, loved enough, worthy enough to say no to requests and people that I loved—so that I could be a yes to me. When really, being a yes to ourselves is not just one of the most important things we can do for ourselves, but it also benefits others.

My trip to India lasted only a couple of weeks. I loved being there, but I felt a stronger pull to go back to California and to face what I was running from. I found a studio apartment right on the sand in the South Bay and signed a six-month lease sight unseen from my computer. It was the first lease I had signed in years, and by signing it, I wasn't just committing to my location—I was also committing to me.

YOU CAN BE A LOVING, SUPPORTIVE PERSON AND SAY NO

When I first landed back in California and word spread that I was back, I was so happy that I no longer owned a car and that I lived just far enough from LA (this was before Uber and Lyft) to be able to give the excuse that I didn't have a ride when I said I couldn't make it to my friends' shows, gatherings, or other invitations. Even though a friend who lived in the same area had offered me her car to use at any time. I was happy to have a legitimate excuse to say no. Sorry, I can't make it! I don't have a car! I would love to hang out, but I don't have a way to get there! Thank you so much for the invite, but I don't have a ride! Soon enough I had to call myself out on that lie as well. The truth was, I didn't **want** to go. I **wanted** to be where I was. I wanted to spend time in my own space, reading, watching shows, writing, walking on the beach, only listening to, eating, and doing what I **wanted** on my own schedule.

I was so nervous the first time I said, "No, I can't make it; I already have plans with myself." But as soon as it came out of my mouth, it felt so right, so freeing, and so true. The truth felt better than making up a lie (even if it was a half-true one). It felt so liberating and rejuvenating to choose me and voice it, instead of hiding it.

Shockingly, when I started to say no and tell the truth about just wanting to have my solo time, my world didn't collapse! No one wrote me off. No one retaliated. No one called me a selfish asshole. Holy shit! I said no without having what seemed like a "real" reason and the world kept spinning? In fact, my honesty led to a deeper mutual respect, understanding, and compassion with my peers and friends. I was allowed to say no and didn't lose anything for doing it. I was allowed to say no and to not feel guilt for it. And it felt so much better than doing things, showing up, going to places that I didn't want to be, because I felt like I *should*. Because that is what I thought a good friend did. Because that is what I thought other people wanted me to do.

> **You can be a good, loving, supportive person and say no.**

> **You can be a good, loving, supportive person and not be self-sacrificing.**

> **You can be a good, loving, supportive person and meet your own needs first.**

In fact, that may make you even more loving, trust-worthy, supportive, *and* compassionate.

And it may even start to inspire those you love to do the same and create an even more honest, open, compassionate, and deeper relationship. Where you are truly able to see each other and hold space for the fullness of each

"You can be a good,
loving, supportive person
and say no."

"You can be a good,
loving, supportive person
and not be
self-sacrificing."

"You can be a good,
loving, supportive person
and meet your own
needs first."

other and your lives. Being a yes to you and prioritizing your own wants does not mean that you don't care about anyone else. It means that you are taking the best care of you, so that they get the best you. It isn't just for you—it is for them too.

> Being a yes to you and prioritizing your own wants does not mean that you don't care about anyone else. It means that you are taking the best care of you, so that they get the best you. It isn't just for you—it is for them too.

THE HARDER LESSON OF SAYING NO EVEN WHEN YOU WANT TO SAY YES

While learning the lesson of allowing myself to say no to things that I didn't **want** to do in order to be a yes to me took giving up everything and fleeing the country— it actually felt easier to get, do, and consistently commit to than what I had to learn next. Sometimes in life we have to say no to even the most awesome invitations and requests in order to take the absolute best care of ourselves and be able to show up for every yes with pure intentions, energy, integrity, and our whole selves. Not a half-assed, bone-tired, used-up version of ourselves.

Two years later, I was nearly halfway through another 18-month tour cycle as the Joyologist, and I was living it up. I absolutely loved my tour family and had shaped my role to create more boundaries, but in some ways, I had also taken on more. It was all good, though, because I *loved* everything that I did! I was good at it and was able to juggle it all with ease! I truly loved every part of my job and had so much fun doing it. In order to do my job of taking care of the artists I worked for, I had to take even better care of myself, and I did! Green juice, green smoothies, super-nutrient-dense meals, yoga, walking, grounding exercises, clearing conversations—I did it all!

On top of the long, long, long days of recording an album, promoting it, and putting on live performances while crisscrossing the globe (sometimes in a new time zone daily), I also said yes to requests for meeting for a drink after, going to the fun party, seeing all the cool things, and more. I was really living up the *yeses* and taking advantage of all the cool opportunities that came my way. They were all **wants**, not *shoulds*! I was living my **wants**! And it landed me in a fancy doctor's office with the classic Hollywood over-exhaustion diagnosis. I had officially hit rock star status, hooked up to IVs and not allowed to leave the trendy LA must-see doctor's office.

I sobbed my eyes out in the hospital bed, realizing that I was going to have to start saying *no* a lot more, even to the things that I wanted to be a *yes* for. Starting with the once-in-a-lifetime trip to Antarctica with Al Gore's Climate Reality Project that I was supposed to be leaving for the next day. Even though I was pretty bad off, the doctor said he would sign the form to clear me to go on the ship. I wanted to go on that trip so freaking bad (I was invited along with the artist I was working with), but I knew it was best for me to stay home and fully recover so that I could show up as the version of me that I wanted to be for myself, and for others, for the next nine months of the tour.

You see, even though I was living out my **wants** *and* taking care of myself, I was sacrificing sleep and alone time that recharged me. Even without the bonus fun yeses

I took on, my life and job itself *was* full. I knew that even though I kept my joy levels high, burning the candle on both ends was making me less creative, less patient, and less caring. And that wasn't the me I wanted to be or to be known as.

FEELING OUT THE YES AND NO

It took me some time to work out a system on how to really know what to say yes to and what to say no to, in order to avoid burnout and the fear of disappointing people. It's easy to say yes in eagerness because you really do **want** to attend the event, see your friend, help out, etc. Then when the day comes around, you are exhausted and no longer feel up to it or just end up always overbooking yourself. You could swap out the "I *should* go because I said I would" feeling by reminding yourself of *why* you said yes and why you do **want** to go. But sometimes by the time the thing comes around, you just really don't have the mental or physical capacity for it. Or life happens and makes it a struggle to do the thing. You could get bad news, have a really bad day, and just really don't feel like your spirit is up for the thing you said yes to.

I mean, how often have you overbooked yourself or said yes to things that you do **want** to do in theory, but then when it comes around, you feel like, "Oh shit, why did I say yes to this?" Or you find yourself wishing for more time in the day. Or feeling like it snuck up on you and you really are just not up for it. You have to own up to seeing that you are not superhuman. You *do* need time to just be, to rest, to recharge, to take care of yourself. So that the world gets to experience the best version of you.

I know it can be hard to say no! But you have to see how important it is to make sure that you can actually fully show up to things you commit to, that you **want** to do, without sacrificing yourself, your health, and your other priorities.

Do you **want** people to get the version of you that is lit up, truly **wants** to be there, and is fully present, or the version of you that is distracted, rushed, anxious, resentful, and/or overtired? Remember, it is not just for your best that you are a yes to you. It is for everyone's best, because it means everyone gets the best, most aligned version of you when they do!

THE SLOW DOWN

One thing that really helped me when I started my path to being way more conscientious of my yeses was slowing down. I initiated a self-mandated hesitation when I received any sort of invitation, ask, or request. *Even if* I immediately felt in my bones that it was a full-on yes. I gave myself a little rule of pausing and not giving a yes or no immediately, but instead giving answers like:

That sounds fun; let me get back to you!

I am interested; let me check my schedule first.

**Thank you so much for the invite;
I will get back to you by _____.**

Just by giving an "I will get back to you" answer, I gave myself more space to explore the event/ask and see what my life would look like on that day, or what it would look like to take on that project/ask. So often people work all

"It is not just for your best that you are a yes to you. It is for everyone's best, because it means everyone gets the best, most aligned version of you when they do!"

week and then fill their weekends and evenings with social activities, not leaving much time for themselves. I am not saying that filling up your schedule is bad or wrong. Some people thrive with consistently full calendars (not me). Always make sure that you are checking in with yourself and **why** you are saying yes.

Is it because you feel it is expected of you?

Is it because you don't want to disappoint them?

Is it because you don't like to be alone?

Is it the fear of missing out?

Is it out of habit?

It's also fine if you don't thrive being alone. I have some friends who are just community people. There is nothing wrong with that. But I also have had many clients who aren't thriving in their friendships but keep choosing to interact with and hang out with people who make them feel like shit. This is often because they are afraid to say no even to the people that they don't enjoy being with. Or, they are afraid of change and of being lonely, even if by being alone they will then be showing up in new spaces in a different way, which could lead to meeting new people.

You can be a good friend and still say no.

You can be a good person and say no.

You can be a good employee and still say no.

You can be a fun, lively, social person and still say no.

You don't have to be available for all the things, all the time.

BE A NONCOMMITTAL/RESPONSIBLE FLAKE

You are allowed to say I don't know! Did you know that? Of course, people would prefer receiving a clear yes or no. But I don't know *is* an acceptable answer, and it is okay to be clear about that. You can be honest. You can be clear that you have a lot going on, and while you want to say yes, you just don't know how you will feel on that day. You can suggest that they get back in touch closer to the date or at a later date. You can ask them when they need a concrete answer by.

> I don't know *is* an acceptable answer.

If you are used to saying yes and to being available, it can feel almost impossible to say no or even I don't know. What helps me with this is to visualize the version of me I would want to attend the event, to be available, to be a yes, and to see if I honestly feel that I will be that person when the date comes. Will I be the rested, alert, relaxed version of me? Or will I be the overtired, anxious, rushed version of me that is fighting off a major headache? How will I feel to be there? Is it the best choice for me and why? Do I have enough space in my life to take on this project? Is it something I really feel aligned with?

And sometimes you just don't know, and you can admit that and give yourself the space to feel it out closer to or on the actual day. You can also be honest that you don't know how you feel and ask for more information that could help you make the best choice for you, and in turn them.

BARGAIN WITH YOURSELF

Sometimes even when it isn't a full body **want**, it still really just doesn't feel right to say no. Either because I do **want** to show my support, or I don't **want** to miss out. In these instances when I can feel a tug toward saying no, but also feel a pull to say yes, I bargain with myself. I make a compromise, going back to my good old any-minutes mantra. If I really don't feel great about being a full no, I remind myself of what fancy NYC magazine editors in chief do (or what I envision they do). I can breeze in and say my hellos, show my support, hug the people I want to hug, have a fully present chat, help out any amount, and then be on my way. I can make an appearance, show up fully, and then leave. I can show up for 5 minutes, 20 minutes, an hour—whatever does it for me—and go.

I do this at events that are meant to be good for me to attend but feel more like a *should* to me. I find a **want** in it and then commit to just 20–30 minutes. Oftentimes I surprise myself by actually enjoying myself and staying longer!

Like I said earlier, make your **want** work for you.

CREATING BOUNDARIES STARTS WITH YOU

Really, all boundaries start, stay, and end with us getting real with ourselves. Even when our boundaries involve how we relate to and show up to other people. They take true commitment on our end. I mean, if they didn't, you wouldn't even have to consider it a boundary. Boundaries can also be purely personal. Creating your own version of balance in your life will mean you are creating boundaries for yourself.

Once my kids started sleeping through the night, I started staying up later, having my own celebration of me time every night. I finally had to institute a be-in-bed-by time and electronic shutdown time, so that I could set myself up to start falling asleep earlier. I can't control what time I fall asleep, but I can at least support myself by getting in bed and shutting down distractions by a certain time. I had to create my own nighttime boundaries to support myself in feeling my best each day. Instead of telling myself I *should* be going to sleep earlier, I got clear on *why* I **wanted** to go to sleep earlier and then created practices to support me in actually doing it.

Sometimes being a yes to you means creating boundaries about conversation topics. For instance, a few years ago I noticed I was triggered when my mom made any mention of my body. Even giving me a compliment about how I looked, like if I had lost weight, really got under my skin. I know she meant well, but it made me aware of how much focus there had been on size, weight, and what my body looked like growing up and into adulthood. This was due to society and my mother's preoccupation with diet and weight loss, which left me with a constant feeling of not being enough. I decided to tell my mom that I was no longer open to talking about or receiving any sort of feedback about my body, including compliments.

I also noticed how much I didn't like talking about my business and work with my mother or with anyone who didn't do something similar. I realized this had gone back to my first career of being a sound engineer. As much as I have always loved my work, I realized that I have never enjoyed talking details and realities about it unless it was with someone who understood the business that I was in.

Otherwise, I felt like I was just getting questions that were odd to me, and when I did give full answers, they never seemed to really care about or understand what I shared, which left me feeling uncomfortable. So I created this new boundary a few years ago that unless the person that I am talking to does or has a background in similar work, I keep my answers light.

How is work going? Good.

How is the writing going? It's going!

**How was that event you were speaking at?
It was awesome. I am grateful I was a part of it.**

You can create boundaries about what you are willing to talk about and with whom. And you are allowed to draw, edit, and erase those lines at any time. You don't even have to tell that person you have the boundary. You can choose to create it and stick with it yourself and create levels of openness with different relationships. You get to choose what you **want** to share with others.

> You can create boundaries about what you are willing to talk about and with whom. And you are allowed to draw, edit, and erase those lines at any time.

My friend Kat says this thing that I love: "I am a thirty-floor building, and some people only get access to the lobby." We don't have to give everyone in our lives the same access. Some people don't actually have the capacity to climb all 30 floors with you. You can love, respect, and appreciate people without giving them full access to all the floors 24/7.

HOW DO YOU FEEL?

You may be thinking, *Yeah, boundaries, great. I know that is something I* should *have, I mean* **want** *to have, but how do I know what boundaries I need?* For me it is in paying attention to how I feel. How do I feel when talking about that topic? How do I feel when I don't do what I **want**? How do I feel when someone gives me a compliment on my body? Paying attention to how I feel gives me access to my own personal treasure map. What do I **want**? What am I doing, ignoring, or participating in that is not contributing to that? What do I not **want**?

> Paying attention to how I feel gives me access to my own personal treasure map.

I noticed I felt like crap when I wasn't getting enough sleep, so I gave myself some sleep boundaries. I noticed I felt anxious and uncomfortable when my mom mentioned my body, even when she was giving me compliments. That led me to creating a boundary. I noticed that when I talked about certain topics with friends that I felt misunderstood or that they weren't even really hearing me, so I created a boundary and chose levels at which to communicate with people. With some people, I feel fully seen, heard, held, and accepted no matter what I am baring my soul about. For some people I stick with shorter answers and enjoy them for who they are and the time we have, without needing to give them access to deeper levels. And these relationships evolve: sometimes they evolve to deeper relationships, sometimes they fade while keeping mutual love and respect.

ARE YOU DISAPPOINTING YOURSELF?

Are you abandoning yourself, not listening to your body, not trusting what you feel because you are worried about disappointing others or about what they will think? So often we put ourselves on the back burner because we don't want to disappoint others—but does that lead us to disappointing ourselves? I was having a phone call with a friend who was due to fly home for the holidays to see her family, but she kept saying that she wasn't sure she wanted to go. She was going through a major life transition with her marriage ending and moving to a new home alone. She was grieving and healing and feeling it all and getting herself set up for the next chapter of her life. She did **want** to see her family after not seeing them all year but was starting to feel that staying put would actually be best for her. She was worried about actually making that choice, though, for fear of disappointing her family, who was looking forward to her visit.

I told her, "You are right: they may be disappointed, but they also love you and want what is best for you. They can be disappointed to not see you *and* support you and your choice at the same time." So often we abandon our own needs, feelings, and intuition, and put others first. **You are worthy of putting yourself first. You are worthy of listening to what you feel. You are worthy of trusting yourself.**

Again and again, remember my favorite word, *and*.

You can trust yourself *and* be loving to others.

You can put your feelings first *and* be considerate of other people's feelings.

They may be disappointed *and* still love you,
believe in you, and support you.

Pay attention to how you feel. Get clear on what you **want** and *why* you **want** it, and **allow yourself to be a yes to you.**

CHAPTER 14

CHOOSE IT OR CHANGE IT.

The reality of living is that shitty stuff happens that *shouldn't* happen.

Your brilliant, amazing friend gets diagnosed with cancer. That *shouldn't* happen. Children lose their parents in a car crash and become separated in foster care. That *should* not happen. You have worked so hard on building a business and unique brand for yourself and then some mega company rips off your biggest phrases and files a cease-and-desist order on you, even though they clearly stole your designs. That *shouldn't* happen. Your co-worker is rude and has little integrity and is always stealing your ideas and saying they are hers. That *shouldn't* happen.

All of these examples are terrible. I wouldn't **want** them to happen to anyone, but things like this happen every day. It is normal, totally acceptable, and necessary to be upset about the shitty stuff that happens in life. What I have realized though (in most cases), is that at some point after the anger, pain, and grief, I am going to have to make a choice so that whatever it is doesn't fully consume me.

We always have a choice. Even if you can't change what already happened or is happening. You always have a choice.

And that becomes clearer every time we question the *shoulds* that come at us. We don't have to choose the *should*. We can make a different choice. And we can also get clearer on why the *should* could be a **want** and end up shifting it to a **want**, making it *our choice*. For me, seeing that I always have a choice is freeing and empowering. But it doesn't always instantly appear like I do have a choice, especially when things are happening that I don't want to happen, that I don't want to have to deal with. That I don't want to face and forge through.

Yet, even when I find myself in circumstances where I can't change what is happening, I remind myself that I still always have a choice in my perspective, on how I handle it, on how I navigate through it. I can be upset and feel that life isn't fair while also choosing to see that this is what is happening. I can **simply choose to accept what is.** By naming what I am feeling, allowing myself to recognize the shitty, and allowing myself to feel what I feel, I get out of reaction mode and go to a more grounded space where I can make reasonable choices to support myself and others. Sometimes it is choosing to make the best of it. Sometimes it is choosing to make a change in my perspective. Sometimes it is just choosing to see that what is happening, is happening. The reminder that I have a choice empowers me and nudges me into action; it empowers me to choose to face what is. It supports me in shifting my attention and/or shifting my attitude so that I can make it through what is happening without it fully taking me down and out.

I've seen it time and time again: people, clients, and loved ones who are resentful of their lives, the past, their jobs, their relationships, and what has happened to them. And I get it! There is a lot that sucks, that is unfair, that I too wish were different. Everything from the way our parents raised us and expressed love or didn't, to being stuck in traffic, to missing your best friend's wedding because your flight was canceled, to a virus taking over the world and shutting it down for months, then a year, then who knows how long. It is not wrong to feel that things *should* be different. To **want** life to unfold exactly as you think it *should*, I mean, exactly as you **want**. But that's life. It happens. To the best of us. To all of us. Some of us more than others, but yes, shitty, unfair stuff will happen even to those people who have everything they want—to those that "have it all." No matter how much planning, intention, and attention you put into something, it still doesn't guarantee that it will go according to plan. And sometimes—sometimes—it *does* go according to plan, and then it is revealed to you that even though you did all the things "right," it still isn't what you **want**, or it still doesn't feel how you imagined it would feel or solve all the problems you thought it would.

Life will amaze us and disappoint us. You are allowed to be upset about it. You are allowed to bitch and complain about it, but at some point, you are going to have to make a choice. A choice to accept it. A choice to change. A choice to change your attitude. A choice as to how you are handling it and making it through. A choice to take action, to raise awareness, to seek support. A choice to choose what is. You can use your anger, frustration, your bitching, and your wishing that it was different to make a change for yourself and perhaps for others too. You can choose acceptance, or action, or both.

> You can use your anger, frustration, your bitching, and your wishing that it was different to make a change for yourself and perhaps for others too. You can choose acceptance, or action, or both.

IT IS WHAT IT IS

Back in my first career as a touring sound engineer, I learned one of my favorite life lessons and mottos that I still use today: "It is what it is." At first take, it may feel kind of depressing and like you are giving up, but I actually found it to be empowering and even hopeful.

You see, when you are on tour, you are often traveling with your own gear to put on the show. Or on smaller tours, you are renting gear or using more of the local venue's gear. But no matter how much of your own gear you are traveling with, each day and each venue will be different. On Thursday you may be loading into a state-of-the-art amphitheater, where the truck just backs up and the road cases easily roll off. The venue sounds amazing, and all the local stagehands and crew are super pros and nice people to work with. Everything is smooth and flows just right.

After the show, you load the gear back up, sleep on the bus as you ride to the next city, and then wake up on Friday to load into a beat-up, funky old club where all the gear has to be carried up three flights of stairs. You have to sacrifice gear and set pieces because you can barely fit anything. The local crew is all hungover (and some still drunk) college kids wearing flip-flops who have no clue what they are doing. It fucking sucks compared to the day before, and the hits keep coming.

But *it is what it is*. You have two choices: whine and complain, and be mopey and mad all day because this day totally sucks. Or accept that *it is what it is* and just freaking choose what is. **You honestly don't have to even put a positive spin on it and tell yourself to make the best of it.** You just accept what is and show up. Every night, no matter how easy the load-in was, how awesome the stagehands were, no matter what—thousands of paying concertgoers were going to show up for the show at 7 P.M. We had to make it happen no matter what. And it was a hell of a lot easier and more enjoyable to just choose to accept it for what it was and laugh through it than to spend my energy bitching, moaning, and complaining about what was not going to be changed.

Living by the "It is what it is" motto empowers me to keep showing up for my life, for what I want, for what I care about, even when it doesn't look easy, pretty, or fun. It reminds me that it is my choice on how I want to experience the day.

IF YOU CAN'T CHANGE IT, CAN YOU CHOOSE IT?

You likely aren't loading gear into venues every day like I was, but I bet you are faced with things you wished were different all the time. Being stuck in traffic is an example that I am pretty sure all of us can relate to and one that allows me to tap back into this practice of choosing.

No one likes to sit in traffic, but traffic happens to all of us. When you are stuck in traffic, you can't do anything about it. But you can accept that you are stuck in traffic. You can choose it.

Imagine that you are stuck in traffic. You are running late for a dinner meeting. You are starving. You are annoyed. You pride yourself on being on time. What do you do? Do you bitch to yourself about the traffic? Do you berate yourself for not leaving earlier or taking another route? You could, but will that make the traffic go away? Will that make sitting in traffic and being late feel better? Will that make you more prepared for whatever it is you are late for? No. As one of my favorite podcast hosts says:

> *What's going to change: the traffic or me?*
> —DAX SHEPARD

You accept that you are stuck in traffic. You *choose* traffic. Traffic is happening, and there is no way out except to wait. You left at the time you left. You took the route that you took. Whatever happened to cause this traffic, already happened. Traffic is what you have in this moment. You can't change that fact, but you can choose it. Instead of being frustrated, annoyed, angry, choose traffic. I mean, you can let yourself have your minute of being pissed, annoyed, and angry, because it is totally necessary to feel your emotions, *and* then choose traffic. Make the best out of it by practicing your pitch for the meeting, listening to a podcast, enjoying music, calling a friend. And sometimes you truly can't find a way to enjoy that waiting time (like when you are stuck in said traffic with two screaming toddlers), but you can still choose that what is happening, is happening, and remind yourself that it won't last forever. It is just what is happening now. Instead of fighting it, accept it.

THIS IS HAPPENING ~~TO ME~~. THIS IS HAPPENING ~~FOR ME~~. THIS IS HAPPENING.

I actually don't think it is healthy to try to put a positive-mindset spin on everything to try to manipulate yourself out of your very real feelings. I mean really, how can you put a positive spin on your most beloved friend getting cancer? You likely can't, and that is one of the reasons that I am not a fan of the "It's not happening *to* me—it's happening *for* me" positive-spin mantra. Don't get me wrong—in some cases, that word swap can really support your mindset and help you get out of your own way. But sometimes that just feels shitty to me. My friend may be dying of cancer, and I am supposed to see how this could be happening *for* me, *for* them, *for* their loved ones? No thank you. Will it make you treasure life and friendships more? Probably. But I still don't love the implication of believing in real time that the shitty thing *had* to happen for you to see that.

I do think in due time we can look back at hard, challenging, and unfair times and see the lessons we learned, how it shaped us, how we reevaluated our priorities, and then find the good that came from them in hindsight. But forcing ourselves to see the positive in hard times can backfire big time and actually may not be the most compassionate way to move through it.

My approach is to move through challenges and challenging times with the simple "This is what is happening" or "It's happening." This allows me to feel what I feel, to see the situation realistically, and to just keep taking steps to make it through it while making space for joy and seeing the good outside of it in my day-to-day.

Back to the example of my most beloved friend getting diagnosed with cancer. I don't have to see how it is happening for my or her best, or imagine the lessons learned and how this experience will shape my life. But I can choose to accept that this is (unfortunately) what is happening and choose to show up and support her as best as I can. The acceptance allows me to show up even more fully instead of either shoving my real feelings aside and ignoring my pain or trying to force myself to see good in it somehow. While we are in it, we can find gratitude for what we do have, the time we get together, the fact that we can FaceTime around the country, and that air travel exists. There is so much to be grateful for—but we don't have to find gratitude *for* the shitty thing while in the shitty thing. Like, I don't have to be grateful that she got cancer to acknowledge how it brought us closer together, get it? When you choose what is, you make space for good and gratitude and joy while also leaving space to feel the other emotions too.

> There is so much to be grateful for—but we don't have to find gratitude *for* the shitty thing while in the shitty thing.

IF YOU CAN'T CHOOSE IT, CAN YOU CHANGE IT?

Sometimes the choice that you need to make is choosing what is, and sometimes it is seeing that you do have a choice and you do **want** to make a change. That could mean a change in your perspective or seeing that you really do **want** to make an actual change in your life and getting out of your damn way to make it!

Let's say you have a co-worker who is constantly getting under your skin. You can start by choosing them. Choose to see that this person is who they are, and they are someone you choose to work with, because you choose to keep this job. Even though, if it were up to you, you would not **want** to spend 40 hours a week with this person, that is what is happening. Accept that they are your co-worker. Choose them as your co-worker.

That may work for you! Every time that you get annoyed, remind yourself that you choose this person as your co-worker. You can even use that Forgiveness Practice when they annoy you and repeat to yourself *I forgive you. I forgive you. I forgive you.* (I have totally used it for this). But if every single day you have to keep reminding yourself to choose them as a co-worker, if every single day you have to remind yourself that "It is what it is" over and over again, drilling it into yourself, it is probably time to make a change.

This could be done by having a conversation with the person. This could be done by talking to a boss to see if you can have fewer interactions with them, switch your schedule, move desks, switch to a different department. This could mean that you make a change in your workplace. Which could seem unfair. Why do I have to change jobs when I am great at my job and love it and this person is ruining it for me? Well, that is your choice. **You can choose to stay where you are and live with the frustrations, or you can choose to make the change and create a new opportunity for yourself.**

Life isn't always fair, but it is a lot more enjoyable when you see that you can choose it or change it instead of just putting up with it. Consider that if you are not choosing to change it, then you are choosing it. Let me say that again:

If you are not choosing to change it, then you are choosing it.

Get real with yourself about why you are not making a change. Is it a fear, a doubt, a *should*? What do you **want**? Are you stopping yourself from having that **want** by staying with what feels easiest? By just putting up with it? Change can be scary because we are so used to just taking the known path of *shoulds*. F those *shoulds*. Choose your **wants**.

> Life isn't always fair, but it is a lot more enjoyable when you see that you can choose it or change it instead of just putting up with it.

CHOOSE YOUR CHOICES

Seeing that we always have a choice is powerful *and* can also create more pressure for us! Which choice do we choose? Sometimes we have so many choices that we just can't decide what to do. We weigh out all the options, read the reviews, ask opinions, acknowledge and account for all the *shoulds*, and see they are options and not musts, but then we have to actually make a choice! I can definitely suffer from decision fatigue and go back and forth, and then when I finally make a choice, I can still wonder, Did I make the right choice? *Should* I have made a different choice?

My personal advice to myself when I am there (and to you when you go there) is:

Choose your choices.

AND

You are always free to choose again.

The reminder of the constant freedom of choice, that I can always choose again, is a huge release and relief to me. Sometimes I just need to kick my own butt back into choosing the choice that I made and to stop doubting, comparing, and worrying. I remind myself *why* I made that choice and then rechoose it. You get to choose for you. You will know when it's time to choose again and when it is time to choose your choice. You just have to quiet the *shoulds* and the doubts, comparisons, and fears they bring! The better you get at F'ing the *shoulds*, the quicker that you will get at coming back to you and allowing yourself to make your own choices, trust your own choices, and choose your own choices. Remember there is no wrong choice. It's all part of life, learning, growing, and evolving.

YOU CAN CHOOSE YOUR PAST

Oftentimes there are parts of our past that we have not accepted. We are ashamed. We have wounds. We realize that we didn't act with integrity. We were immature. We were naive. We feel taken advantage of. We were wronged. We were used. We were attacked. We are understandably upset about what we did and what was done to us. Whatever it is, we all have bumps in our past that can make us cringe at the memories. The next time that you wince at a memory from your past, ask yourself, What if I tried to choose it? Choose that it did happen. Accept that you cannot go back and change it. Instead of fighting it, trying to wish it away, punishing yourself, and letting *should* control your past—choose it. Accept that it is a part of your past and then work on moving forward from there. Choose your past, because it is already yours. It already happened.

This is another power of choice that continues to give me healing and freedom: accepting that what already happened, already happened. Choosing what already happened, whether it was something that happened to you or a past choice that you made. When I find myself wishing my past away, cringing at what happened, feeling resentful, and more—the reminder that I can choose my past gives me some instant relief and healing. Choosing your past doesn't mean that you are saying it was right. It doesn't mean that you would make that same choice for yourself today or that you are happy that it happened how it did. It doesn't even mean you are grateful for the lessons you learned from it.

> What already happened, already happened. By simply accepting that it did happen it supports me in forgiving, healing, and moving forward.

By choosing to see that what happened, already happened, I am simply accepting that it did happen. Which supports me in forgiving, healing, and moving forward. Acceptance for me is healing and allows me to tend to my feelings, my experiences, and what I **want** for my now and my future. Again, I am not trying to put a positive spin on it, but to hold space for the part of my life it inhabited and to make space for my full humanness and perhaps other people's too.

I mean, you can't hide from your past. And choosing your past does not mean that you are choosing it for your present or your future. You are not saying that the wrongs were right. You are simply accepting that what happened, happened.

And just like it supports me to choose my past, it supports me to choose my parents. Many of us can have deep wounds from how we were raised. We wish our parents had showed up for us differently, done things differently, put different values and messages into our heads. But what if you choose your parents as the parents they were, as they are. What if you choose that your mom/dad/caretaker is your mom/dad/caretaker and they raised you how they raised you? Again, that doesn't mean that you are happy about it or that you approve of the choices that they made.

It is making peace with what is, because it is. We can't change our past, but we can change how we relate to it. We cannot change other people and how we think they *should* express their love and support. We can express it to them, but we cannot change them. So sometimes the most powerful and healing thing that we can do is choose them as they are. My mom is my mom. I choose her as she is. My dad was my dad. I choose him as he was.

You don't have to reunite with them. You don't have to have any sort of "I choose you" conversation with them. This is for you, but it may work to shift your relationship and memories of them too.

"We can't change our past,
but we can change
how we relate to it."

YOU GET TO CHOOSE

Your past, you cannot change, but your present, you can. You can choose each present moment. You get to choose the tasks on your **want-to-do** list. You get to choose to be in your relationship or to change it. Even on those days that you don't love your job, you get to choose your job and what it does for you. And if you cannot choose it, you can change it. You can. Believe that you can.

If it is constantly hard to choose what you are doing and what you have, empower yourself to change it. If it is consistently a challenge to choose your partner for who they are, make a change. If it is consistently a challenge to choose your job, make a change. If you struggle to choose it, if you struggle to change your attitude about it, **see that you have the choice to make a change.**

Choose it. Change it. Those are your choices. Take ownership of your life. Even when things happen that are out of your control, like traffic, you can choose it.

should-to-**want** choice, I was choosing me. I was support-ing me. I was coming home to the me of the present and appreciating, acknowledging, and celebrating her. And every time, still to this day, it feels so fucking freeing and empowering to be reminded that this is *my* life, and I am allowed to make my own choices and do things my own way. This is *your* life, and you are allowed to make *your* own choices and do things *your* own way.

I hope you have started to notice yourself how much *shoulds* weigh on us (consciously and unconsciously) and really have us self-sabotaging and in a state of questioning our worth all day long. But we do not have to fall victim to them! Every single day, in the smallest and also in huge ways, I am strengthening my self-worth muscle by F'ing the *shoulds* and choosing my **wants**, by giving myself this permission. I am no longer blindly following the path of *shoulds* that had been invisible to me before. By pausing to explore my **wants**, my thoughts, my beliefs, and seeing that I am allowed to choose, it opens me up to the limit-less possibilities that do exist, but that so often we are not seeing. Or we see the possibilities, but we feel that those possibilities cannot possibly be available for us—those are for other people. Allowing yourself to see your **wants** and allowing yourself to have **wants** will continue to allow you to bulldoze through the walls that you inadvertently created for yourself and that society has created for you.

Things as small as wearing only a sports bra to work out in—even just at home! The *shoulds* of the world had me believing that you *should* only show your stomach (even the smallest bit) if you are super lean and svelte. This may seem small, but it is another way that I recently discovered that I was implanting in myself that I wasn't

"This is *your* life,
and you are allowed
to make *your* own choices
and do things
your own way."

enough—that I wasn't accepting myself. So, even when I **wanted** to wear one to exercise in because of how hot and sweaty I got in my garage, I had this deeply embedded *should* fucking with me and making me feel like I wasn't enough, that I wasn't allowed to. Yet I **wanted** to wear it. Finally, I F'ed that *should* and reminded myself: I am allowed to wear this regardless of my size, my weight, my age. I get to decide. I am allowed! And the more I allowed myself to do it, the more I got comfortable in my own flesh, no matter how fleshy I was. Which eventually led me to wearing only a sports bra out for a hike and then to a hot yoga class and then to feeling more confident in a bathing suit at a hotel pool. All these years I had spent telling myself I shouldn't show my skin and guess what? NO ONE cared. NO ONE was bothered.

Even the dishes! Doing the damn dishes! It still feels so freeing to me, to this day, when I make the choice to leave the dishes for the morning. The choice is so against what I was raised to do and what I feel like I *should* choose, *and* yet I don't feel shame or like I am lazy or a slob or wrong for doing so. When I start to question my choice and wonder what so-and-so would think if they saw these dirty dishes left overnight, I remind myself *why* I am choosing to leave the dishes to do later and that *I am allowed* to leave the dishes until the morning, when I have more energy and time.

During that first no-*should* summer, when these internal debates of choosing the *should* versus the **want** came up, I was honestly feeling a little unsettled by giving myself all of these choices. The reminder that *I am allowed* empowered me and rooted me back within myself.

Each day, from morning to night, as I navigated from *shoulds* to **wants**, I had this arm-pumping feeling soaring from me that I am allowed!

I am allowed to say no.

I am allowed to wake up when I **want**.

I am allowed to skip yoga today.

I am allowed to eat pizza.

I am allowed to like quiet nights at home alone.

I am allowed to say no to an invitation to hang out with someone I love to choose a quiet night at home.

I am allowed to speak up.

I am allowed to send the e-mail asking for help.

I am allowed to take this time off.

I am allowed to not know what I want to do next.

I am allowed to tell them how I felt about what they said/did.

I am allowed to change my mind.

I am allowed to listen to my gut.

I am allowed to enjoy this song, even though it's pop music and I thought I didn't like pop music.

I am allowed to wear leggings 90 percent of the time.

I am allowed to be this size and accept and love myself.

I am allowed to live my life my way.

You are allowed to live your life your way.

YOU WILL BE JUDGED NO MATTER WHAT—
SO DO YOU

In our society, just existing and experiencing life is looked down on once you become an adult. One of the first questions people ask when first meeting someone is, "What do you do?" It can feel like it is only acceptable to not have a job or to be in between jobs if you are a stay-at-home parent or are married and your spouse provides for you or you are independently wealthy. Yet people will still judge you for those reasons. I mean really, what can't you be judged for? You are judged for being a working parent. You are judged for being a stay-at-home parent. You are judged because you have money to support you. You are judged because you don't have much money. **This is why it is so important to be real with yourself about what you believe to be true about you.**

Not just once in my life, but several times, I have chosen to exist and live in the "I don't know." When I gave up my dream tour after my dad passed away, that was one thing. It felt more self-explanatory to other people. I was grieving and looking for a life change, but even then, people would be uncomfortable when I would reply to their "What do you do?" questions with versions of, "I am taking time off to figure out what I **want** to do next." Even in times of major grief and tragedy, we are programmed to just keep going. I mean, you aren't supposed to take a leave. You aren't supposed to quit your job just to have space to feel. (Supposed to's are versions of *shoulds*, if you haven't figured that out yet.) You keep working and working and working until you retire or die. Bullshit. You have to stop letting other people's judgments and *shoulds* stop *you* from trusting yourself.

That wasn't the only time, though, that I simply allowed myself to exist for months at a time without knowing for how long or what would be next. I wasn't always financially set up for this either. I am not promoting it, but I have opened zero-percent-interest credit cards many times to float me when I was existing in these times of just being, allowing, and waiting to see what I wanted to do next. The biggest chunk of time I took "off" (not including the year of grief), I was able to live off some savings I had stored up from one of the 18-month tour cycles I did. On that break I knew that I was ready to stop touring, but I also wasn't 100 percent clear on what to focus on next for work to support me that also fulfilled me. I think I went more than six months without a job or income, and I loved every single day of it. I didn't *should* on myself once about it. Other people, though, just couldn't understand it. What do you do all day? What are your goals? What is your timeline? What's next for you? They wanted answers, because me not having what they thought of as a good enough answer made them uncomfortable. They felt I *should* have a job. I *should* know. I *should* have a plan.

> Stop letting other people's judgments and *shoulds* stop *you* from trusting yourself.

Almost daily I would get the questions from friends, loved ones, past co-workers, and others that would nudge the *shoulds* at me, and I would keep reminding myself that *I am allowed* to live in the "I don't know." *I am allowed* to simply experience life, to just enjoy the day-to-day beauty that we miss out on by going, going, going, to allow myself to stay open to life and what I would want to do next. Were there financial and other risks involved in that? Yep, and I accepted that. Eventually, after months of rest and restoration and no forcing, I moved forward with some of the many ideas that had surfaced to create my *Own Your Awesome* affirmation deck, launch coaching programs, and more. And I did it all from a pure place of **want**. Not because I *should* be doing something, or I *should* get back to work. Not because I *should* make the most of the attention I had received as a Joyologist to the stars . . .

It's so mind-boggling to me how much we fight doing what we need—what we **want**. From making a career change to allowing ourselves to rest, or to simply be in our lives and enjoy them, without feeling like we *should* be doing something else or doing more. At this point in my life, with kids to support and not much savings, I don't have the option to only focus on myself and to not bring in any income for months at a time. Yet I *can* allow myself to rest, to embrace the ebbs and flows of life, to make space for daily wonder, and not be pushing to go, go, go all the time. Do I **want** to make more money to provide more security for myself and my family? Absolutely, but I also don't **want** to miss out on actually being in my life and enjoying it, while I get the chance to be living it. And I don't want that for you either.

Are you allowing yourself to be yourself? Are you allowing yourself to truly enjoy your life? Are you allowing yourself to truly nurture yourself? Are you allowing yourself to truly rest? Or are you *shoulding* yourself to keep going, to have your answer, your next step, to just keep pushing? What are you striving for, if not to allow yourself to live your life while you are in it?

We don't realize how much we are living into *shoulds*, into expectations (other people's, society's, and our own), into routines that don't serve us until we create a conscious awakening to it. We don't realize that how we feel about ourselves and how much our self-worth is tied up in our *shoulds* until we start to examine our feelings and where the *shoulds* are coming from.

All day long you have the choice to give yourself permission to look within and honor the current you and the future you or to stay in line with the past versions of you and what you thought and were told you *should* want/do/be. You have the power to stop limiting your life choices. To stop judging yourself. To stop telling yourself that you aren't enough. To stop abandoning yourself each day in even the smallest of ways. The little daily stuff matters. The little stuff is the source of the big stuff. Life goes by so fast! Live it your way! Allow yourself to truly *live* and enjoy *your* life.

You are allowed to wear what brings you joy,
no matter what size you are.

You are allowed to be a walker and not a runner.

You are allowed to choose the restaurant.

You are allowed to love pop music and boy bands.

You are allowed to enjoy reality TV.

You are allowed to spend your money
on things that bring you joy.

You are allowed to enjoy living with roommates.

You are allowed to want a simple life.

You are allowed to want more for yourself.

You are allowed to quit the job that was your dream job to take one for less income that doesn't cause you stress and leaves you space to truly live your life outside of work.

You are allowed to ask for a raise.

You are allowed to say no (with no explanation).

You are allowed to move on from a friendship that rarely leaves you feeling good about yourself.

You are allowed to want different things from those you love.

You are allowed to break off your engagement, even if it means disappointing family and you paid all the deposits.

You are allowed to give up the career you built to become a stay-at-home mom.

You are allowed to enjoy working full-time and being a mom.

You are allowed to not have kids, even if everyone tells you what a great parent you would be.

You are allowed to love who you love.

You are allowed to rest without feeling like you have to earn it.

You are allowed to forgive yourself.

You are allowed to celebrate yourself.

You are allowed to express yourself.

You are allowed to have **wants**.

You are allowed to do the **wants**.

You are allowed to see your worth.

You are allowed.

Yes, people may very well judge you for your choices, for who you are, for what you do, for what you wear, for all of it. But that isn't about you. That is their own shit, their own programming, their own attachment to *shoulds*. It isn't about you. You will be judged by someone, somewhere, no matter what—so do you. Leave the judging to other people. Allow yourself to be yourself instead of you being the one who is judging you for being you.

YOU ARE ALLOWED TO FEEL WHAT YOU FEEL

Something that I have noticed in my coaching work and in just being a human is that we can try to *should* ourselves out of our feelings. Either because those feelings are uncomfortable or because we feel that we *shouldn't* feel them or that we *should* be over it.

Maybe you are going through a breakup, and you are the one who chose to end things, yet you find yourself missing them, you feel sad, you feel lost, you feel alone; maybe you doubt your choice to break up. But you try to *should* yourself out of feeling those feelings because you made the choice to break up.

Maybe you are feeling hurt, offended, left out because your friends did something and didn't invite you. It hurts, but you feel petty for feeling that way so you try to *should* yourself out of what you are feeling. You want to be a bigger person. You know it is really no big deal. But you do feel hurt.

"You will be judged by someone, somewhere, no matter what—so do you. Leave the judging to other people. Allow yourself to be yourself instead of you being the one who is judging you for being you."

Maybe you are struggling, but you feel that you don't have the right to feel like life is hard because of all that you do have and how so many people have it worse. Invalidating your own struggles and feelings won't help you or the people who have it worse than you.

Not allowing yourself to feel your feelings doesn't make them go away. *Shoulding* them away or trying to wave a magic positivity wand over your feelings won't make them disappear. You can't fake your feelings into reality.

My life, my heart, my compassion, my resilience opened up so much more when I finally started to allow myself to feel what I was feeling. Even if those feelings could have been looked at as petty. Even if what I was going through could have been seen as so much less than what others were struggling with. Even if I really didn't **want** to feel that way. They were my feelings, and by trying to *should* myself out of them instead of actually acknowledging what I was feeling and getting curious about it, they didn't really go away or get healed. They were just pushed down inside, where they were eroding and eating away at me.

I'm human and so I can feel pangs of jealousy when I see someone get an opportunity that I want. In the past I would feel wrong, or like I was a bad person for feeling jealous, so then I would pile shame on top of those feelings and try to just force myself out of my feelings. Now, I acknowledge what I am feeling and explore it. Coming to myself compassionately, instead of telling myself I am wrong to feel that way, I am then able to take those feelings of jealousy and look deeper. I open myself up to see that this person getting what I want is proof that what I **want** is possible not just for them, but for me also. My jealousy then turns into celebration and motivation. I become motivated to get my own butt in gear, to keep going, to keep showing up for what I want and I am able to truly celebrate them.

By tuning in to and giving a name to what you are feeling, you actually neutralize the emotion and are able to take a step out of it to see what is really happening within you. When you're present to what you are feeling, you don't feel it more; you actually lessen the weight and begin to take back the power from the emotions instead of trying to push them away and outrun them. As I guided you in Chapter 4, try acknowledging them instead of trying to push past them.

ALLOW THE DUPLICITY

You are also allowed to feel more than one thing at once! Sometimes when people are grieving, they feel like they are wrong for allowing themselves to experience any joy. We aren't often shown that it is natural to be both distraught and to experience joy at the same time. Or we try to turn the frown upside down and push ourselves to only feel the "good" feelings, which isn't actually helpful. Feeling more than one thing is completely natural and healthy.

You can feel upset *and* grateful.

You can feel nervous *and* excited.

You can feel stress *and* at ease.

You can be sad *and* feel joy.

You can be scared *and* at peace.

Making yourself wrong or telling yourself you are only allowed to feel one way or the other is ridiculous. It is not supporting you but limiting you.

Allow yourself to feel it all. Even if your brain tries to tell you that it's wrong. That's just the *shoulds* messing with you again!

YOU HAVE PERMISSION TO MAKE AND BREAK YOUR OWN RULES

We are so quick to judge ourselves and make ourselves feel like we are doing "it" wrong. It is like we are following some invisible set of rules. Who made these rules? Why do we keep putting our life choices in the hands of others? Why do we keep looking outside of ourselves for approval, for validation, for acknowledgment? Why do we so often default to caring more about what "they" will think, instead of getting clearer and honoring what we think? Who is this invisible "they" that we are allowing to run everything from the smallest details of our lives to the most important and the most intimate? Why do we keep overlooking and sacrificing ourselves?

What invisible rules are you following?

Who made them?

How are they serving you?

You are allowed to make your own choices. You are allowed to move beyond the *shoulds* and to ask yourself, "What do I **want**?" You actually do have choices, and you are allowed to choose what you **want.** It is not selfish! And your choices also don't have to be permanent! You have permission to make your own rules. You have permission to break your own rules. We are all evolving, always. You are allowed to change your mind. Remind yourself that the rules you are following aren't actually rules; they are choices.

> You have permission to make your own rules. You have permission to break your own rules.

BREAK OUT OF THE BOX

Have you noticed how, for some reason, we are wired to believe we must be either/or? How we try to put ourselves in boxes? How we limit ourselves by not making space and allowing the duplicity and complexity of ourselves? For years, I didn't allow myself to read novels because I told myself that it wasn't spiritual. For years, I didn't allow myself to like pop music because I was attached to this image I had of myself as a cool rock chick. When we let go of those nonsensical lines we have drawn and the boxes that the world tries to put us in, we become so free! We allow joy to flow. We allow bliss to be present. We allow ourselves to accept, be, and thrive as our complicated, ever-evolving selves.

> When we let go of those nonsensical lines we have drawn and the boxes the world tries to put us in, we become so free!

Get yourself more acquainted with my favorite word, *and*. Ah, *and*—it feels so expansive and embracing. Where can you make space for more *and* in your life? Where can you knock down walls and start to open up some doors?

You can be all about natural health and wellness *and* take medication that supports you.

You can be a badass, independent changemaker *and* need support.

You can break up with someone who you know is not the ideal partner for you *and* love, miss, and appreciate them.

You can be spiritual *and* thoroughly enjoy reading novels.

You can be intellectual *and* love reality TV.

You can love someone *and* want space from them.

Allow yourself to fully own all parts of yourself, and allow that for others too.

INSTANT STRESS RELIEF

Just another major bonus: by seeing and giving myself permission, by seeing that *I am allowed*, I instantly release so much *stress* from my body, my nervous system, and my mind. It's like a magic little instant relief button.

It feels like a magical glowing orb coming out of my body, expanding my mind and my heart and relaxing my soul and nervous system. And we always have access to this button, to this glowing orb of self-allowance and self-love (it may just be hidden under layers and layers of doubts, shame, comparison, and *shoulds*).

You awaken your own self-worth by choosing yourself. By trusting yourself. By allowing yourself to do what is best for you and seeing that in the end it will benefit all. Because the world will get the most connected, authentic, honest you who is showing up with your full heart and integrity.

The whole point of this book is for you to look beyond the limitations that you may have set for yourself unconsciously and to continuously rip apart the conditioning society has put on us. I **want** you to give yourself true freedom and permission to explore possibilities, to dream beyond the limitations that have been set for you, to listen deeper to yourself and to trust yourself. By doing the daily work of releasing the *shoulds*, you will be freeing yourself again and again.

CHAPTER 16

~~I SHOULD.~~
~~I WANT TO. I WILL.~~
I AM!

Our words matter. Our choice of words matters. They aren't just words. They are intentions. They are proclamations. But so often we spit them out and keep going with little thought. And that is the main takeaway of this book. That by paying attention to just that one word—*should*—you are tuning in to and getting clear with yourself, your intentions, and your whys. You are getting clear on who you are, what you **want**, and why you **want** it. *All day long. Every day.* Because that is how often the *shoulds* come at us. All day long. Every day.

We can't control the thoughts that come into our minds, but we can get better at catching and transforming them. It is part of our human DNA to have doubts, fears, judgments, worries, and more. We don't have to beat ourselves up for that. We didn't fail; we aren't less than. **We can greet our very real thoughts and feelings with love** and listening, but we also don't have to believe everything that we think.

The most valuable thing that I have gotten from eliminating the word *should* is the mindfulness it gave me. By focusing on one word, it opened my eyes, ears, and nerve endings to the way I use words in general and the very real impact they have. By focusing on that one word, I was able to tune in to what I am thinking and feeling, all day long. It didn't happen overnight, it is a continuous practice (as evidenced by this entire book). But stay the course, stay mindful, and keep F-ing those *shoulds*!

THE NEXT STEP TO ACTIVATE YOUR WANTS

Over and over in these chapters I share the power of shifting from *shoulds* to **wants**. By shifting from *should* to **want**, you are making an intentional shift, but it can still leave you (and me) unactionable.

You get clear on what you **want** and what you don't **want**. You get clear, or clearer, on *why* you **want** what you **want** and/or *why* you had been motivated to do the *should*. And hopefully it motivates you to go in the direction of your **want**. But, of course, we may still experience mental and real-life roadblocks. Just naming a **want** doesn't mean that you automatically believe that it is possible for you to get into gear and get it done with the snap of your fingers. Doubts will still surface; judgments will still come up. Our minds will get creative and make it harder to follow through. They will tell us that we don't have time, or they will default to saying no to prevent us from showing up or believing in ourselves and on and on. Oh, and of course there is just the fullness of our lives to distract us.

What I have used for years to combat these interfering thoughts and to call myself into the believing and the doing are affirmations. You have likely heard of affirmations and maybe already use them. They aren't new, and they don't belong to one person. An affirmation is a statement that calls you into believing what it is that you **want** to believe about yourself. They most commonly start with "I am." They use language to motivate, empower, inspire, nurture, and heal.

Definition of Affirmation:

the act or an instance of affirming; state of being affirmed.

the assertion that something exists or is true.

something that is affirmed; a statement or proposition that is declared to be true.

confirmation or ratification of the truth or validity of a prior judgment, decision, etc.

But they too can lead to no real change in your thoughts, beliefs, and actions. **In fact, trying to use affirmations that feel too big could make you feel worse about yourself!** I mean, if you have been led to believe your whole life that in order to be loved and accepted you had to be a certain body size and look a certain way, and then one day you start to say, "I am enough as I am right now," it may be hard for your mind and heart to believe. It may be too big of a statement to digest at first if you have been telling yourself you are not enough for as long as you can remember. Even though it is absolutely true. You are enough right now, no matter what you look like, no matter what your size is, no matter what your income or bank account or relationship status is.

WRITE IT OUT

Back in Chapter 5, I mentioned how Julia Cameron's "morning pages" broke me of being so precious about journaling and actually got me to put words on the page in order to support myself in healing and feeling through my feelings. Following this "let it flow" format is what ultimately led me to my approach of creating and using affirmations.

In *The Artist's Way*, Cameron directs us to just put pen to page and vent it all out, without worrying about making any sense or following a straight line of thought. She instructs to handwrite three full pages. Just keep going until you fill the pages. Even if you are just writing, "I don't know what to write," keep writing. There is no need to write in paragraphs; literally just word vomit onto the page. Be fully honest about your thoughts, feelings, actions, and attitudes, and also allow yourself to jump from what you are feeling to remembering an errand you want to run. Allow it to be a total stream of consciousness. It doesn't have to make sense or follow any writing rules. This isn't a Dear Diary entry that you will come back to years from now. You can tear it up when you are done and never look at it again.

Allow it to be jumbled and to jump around like this:

My body hurts. Oh shit, I keep forgetting to schedule that appointment. I still can't get over what Brittany said about me. I mean, I know she has had it rough, but I think that she is handling this all wrong. What am I going to eat for lunch today? I am worried about how I am going to pay my rent next month. I have this month covered but nothing set up for sure next month.

And on and on for three pages.

This practice feels so liberating to do, *but* when I first started it, I had a really hard time being honest with myself. It was easy for me to write about the things that I wanted to do, to dream, to do a brain dump of to-dos and processing about other people. But any time that one of my own doubts, fears, stresses, or worries started to come up and out, I hesitated. *Wait.* I can't write those down! If I write those down that will make them real. I am a positive badass who can do anything that I put my mind to! I don't have doubts and fears.

LOLOLOLOL. Oh dear, sweet, younger Tricia.

I worried that I would be manifesting it as my reality if I wrote it down. Would I be calling in my fears if I admitted to them? Would I be forever plagued by my doubts if I gave them attention? I wanted to dismiss and blow past those thoughts that we are taught to label as negative. But what I allowed myself to see was, if even an inkling of those thoughts was coming up for me, they already were real. They were living within me, and running from them, ignoring them, hiding them away was *not* going to cure them. Me pretending (to myself and to others) that I only thought positive, supportive, encouraging things was absolute bullshit and was actually holding me back, as I wasn't actually facing what I felt and feared.

It was so hard for me to start letting those things go onto the page. It was truly a challenge to begin to even dip my toe into admitting, even to myself, that doubts and fears and judgment and mean thoughts existed within me! But when I started to let myself see it and name it, I was then given the path to do the work to actually show up for myself instead of just glossing over it all with positive platitudes. It forced me to see and face the things that I wanted to push away. So that I could then address them head on with compassion and curiosity as I did the work to shift them. And by facing them, I was actually giving myself a stronger ground to stand on.

MY AFFIRMATION FRAMEWORK

This is where I got the framework that I use for creating affirmations that actually serve, empower, and heal me in my life daily. By getting real with myself about what I am feeling, what I am fearing, what I am struggling with, what I am judging, where I am comparing, where I am struggling with that pesky not enough-ness, and more. Once I face it, I can then ask myself, "Is this really what I want to believe? What do I want to believe?" This framework starts similar to what I shared in Chapter 7, when we were tackling inner judgment, but takes it one step further.

1. What am I telling myself?

The first step for me is to name what I am thinking, believing, and/or feeling. This is so, so, so huge and important! I am pretty sure I have said that over and over again already in this book, and that is because it's *the truth*. The naming of the belief, doubt, fear, worry, emotion, etc. itself creates a major clearing and lifts the weight of it away. It truly has the opposite reaction than you would think. I mean, isn't it easy to guess that by giving these thoughts your attention, you would embody them more? But really, you are bringing them to the light by naming them instead of allowing them to keep hiding in the shadows. For example:

I need to lose weight.

I never feel like I am enough,
that I am doing enough.

I am pissed and jealous that everyone else
keeps getting the opportunities that I want.

I am so behind.

2. What do I want to believe?

Once you name it, you can then question it. And the biggest question to ask yourself is, "What do I **want** to believe?" Just like I did when I was judging myself before my NYC photo shoot back in Chapter 7. You get to remind yourself that you are not stuck with that thought, belief, doubt, fear, worry, shame, etc. What do you **want** to believe?

I **want** to believe that my worth has nothing
to do with my weight and that I can
accept myself right now as I am.

I **want** to believe that I am enough,
and I do enough.

I **want** to believe that I will get a similar
opportunity soon.

I **want** to believe that I am right on time and that
everything I have done in my life and have been
through so far has set me up for my future.

> You get to remind yourself that you are not stuck with that thought, belief, doubt, fear, worry, shame, etc. What do you **want** to believe?

3. Create your very own *now*-tense statement

Then you turn your **wants** into *now*-tense statements to call yourself into embodying what it is you **want** to believe. Oftentimes this is simply swapping out **want** for "I am" and then filling in the blank, creating it as if it is already so. Sometimes it is taking out the **want** and simply putting a *My* or *I* at the start to make the statement true in the now. You are creating a statement that takes what you **want** and makes it into a current fact.

> **My worth has nothing to do with my size.**
> **I accept myself as I am.**

> **I am enough. I am doing enough.**
> **There is no magical "enough" place to get to!**

> **My opportunity is already on its way!**

> **I am right on time. Everything that I have done**
> **in my life and have been through so far**
> **has set me up for my future. I am right on time.**

Get creative and use language that feels exciting and empowering to *you* for it to be the most effective for you. You **want** the statements to feel all tingly. Like they make you **want** to jump up and say *yes*, even if they still feel a little uncomfortable. For example, wanting to believe in yourself could be any of these variations or another that speaks to you:

> **I am a badass who can do anything**
> **I put my mind to.**

> **I believe in all of the possibilities that**
> **do exist for me.**

> **I am invincible.**

Or if you are concerned about finances, it could vary like these:

I am a magical money maker.
Money is always coming my way.

I am a badass at making money.
People love to give me money.

I am provided for.

I am abundant.

TRANSITIONAL AFFIRMATIONS— FOR WHEN YOU JUST CAN'T GET THERE

Sometimes, though, creating a statement to enforce what you do **want** to believe still doesn't land or feel very reality based. I mean, let's look at the last example about struggling financially. Creating an affirmation to soothe your financial worries will likely vary based on your situation. People with high-paying corporate jobs can worry about money. Independent contractors who don't always have steady work can worry about money and where their work is coming from next month. People working multiple jobs, living paycheck to paycheck, can worry about money. People who lost their jobs months ago and haven't gotten a new interview due to the state of the economy (having nothing to do with their abilities or putting themselves out there) can be worried about money.

Let's be real: if you are unemployed during a pandemic with no end in sight, sitting around saying, "I am abundant" (or any of the others I suggested) may not do it for you.

This is where what I call transitional affirmations come in. You still go through the above process, naming what you are struggling with and then asking yourself what you want to believe. Or instead of using what you want to believe, you create a statement to use that feels supportive. But instead of an "I am"–type statement, you are going to start it with, "Even though [enter the struggle]" and then add the **want**/supportive statement. The structure is different from the types of phrases we created above.

Here are some examples:

Even though I am worried about how I will pay my bills next month, I know I am supported.

Even though I am worried about money, I am showing up daily for the opportunities that do exist for me.

Even though I am worried about money, I am grateful for my health.

Even though I am not confident in my body, I am working to love myself deeper.

Even though I am not confident in my body, I am grateful for what my body does for me and how it supports me.

I got this language from the EFT tapping modality, and I feel like it is the most compassionate and reality-based language for affirmations, especially if you are new to using them this way, to actually help you face and transform what *you* are struggling with.

You can also cut out the "even though" and simply state what it is you are struggling with *and* affirm yourself. Like this:

I am worried about how I will pay my bills next month, *and* I know this time in my life isn't permanent.

I am not comfortable in my body, I want to be in better shape, *and* I am working on loving myself as I am right now.

I am worried I will always be alone, *and* I acknowledge that I am worthy of love.

Repeating these (or any affirmation) won't magically make money appear in your bank account, heal your heartbreak, or erase your fears. *But* it shuts down your worry, fear, doubt, and comparison feedback cycle, has you approaching your real thoughts with love, *and* makes space for hope, gratitude, compassion, dreams, and more.

TIPS TO ACTUALLY USE THEM

As I mentioned above, creating and repeating these powerful statements is not like waving a magic wand over your life. But they aren't pointless. They aren't a waste. They aren't just a toxic positivity brainwashing exercise. You can intercept the thoughts that have a hold on you, question them, and replace them with your new affirmations. Over and over again. Stop ignoring what you are telling yourself and believing. Stay curious and see that you aren't stuck with those thoughts or beliefs, no matter

"Stop ignoring what you
are telling yourself and
believing. Stay curious and
see that you aren't stuck with
those thoughts or beliefs,
no matter how long they
have been around
and how hard they try
to come back."

how long they have been around and how hard they try to come back.

Face yourself; allow yourself to believe in yourself, to love yourself, to nurture yourself, and to forgive yourself. Affirmations will work—if you work them.

Now for my hot tips on how to implement them every day. The ideal way to use them is in the moment to turn our thoughts around. But even then, we may need more work to override the fears, doubts, worries, and stress that are implanted in us. These are my favorite ways to make affirmations a part of my daily life.

Write It Out

Write your affirmation of the moment over and over again, spending time with it and claiming it for yourself. You can add this to your three pages of freewriting if you try out the journaling style I prefer. Fill up some of the pages with affirmations if you get stuck or end your writing that way. Or it can be an individual practice. One way I keep this up is to leave a notepad or open journal and pen next to my bed in a place that I can't miss it (you could even leave it on your bed). Each day and night (when I remember), I write down at least three "I am" statements of what I **want** to believe, feel, and call in. It only takes a few minutes and it wakes me up to what I want and who I am.

Mirror Work

Say the affirmations to yourself in the mirror! It can be so uncomfortable at first, but it is so powerful! My favorite tip is to make a habit out of saying affirmations every time that you go to the bathroom. Normally, you do your thing and then wash your hands, and there is nearly always a mirror there. Instead of going into what many people default to—criticizing your skin, hair, face, outfit, etc.—meet your own eyes in the mirror as you wash your hands and repeat your affirmation(s) to yourself. You can say them out loud, if alone, or to yourself if in a public space. Even silently, you can meet your own eyes and say these things that you **want** to believe to yourself. You can also write affirmations on your mirrors! Dry erase markers wipe off easily so that you can change them up as often as you like! This is a habit that you can commit to daily, because you go to the bathroom daily, right?

Partner Work

This is really effective, moving, and special! Find an affirmation buddy. Maybe a co-worker, friend, roommate, partner, etc. You say your affirmation out loud to them using "I" language, and then they say it back to you in "You" language, back and forth, so that you have the power of your own voice saying it and you get to hear it being said back to you! Warning, this can be super emotional! When I first did it years ago, I sobbed every time. Hearing it said back to me just really hit me in a way that I was able to truly feel it to my core and allow myself a deeper possibility to believe it. Do it back and forth for a good amount of times and then switch!

I am worthy of my dreams.—You are worthy of your dreams. (Back and forth).

I am enough right now as I am.—You are enough right now as you are. (Back and forth.)

IT IS MAGIC, I TELL YOU!

Passwords!

I love to make my passwords into affirmations of what I want to believe or of what I am calling in! That way, every time that I log on to my laptop, credit card accounts, membership sites, etc. I am reminded, "Oh yeah, that is what I **want** to believe. That is what I **want** for myself. That is what I am calling in." Get creative with upper and lower case letters, numbers, and characters. Make it fun— and secure.

THIS IS THE END— BUT IT NEVER ENDS.

When I go a little while without doing yoga and then do it again, it feels amazing to be opening up my stiff joints and muscles, *and* it brings a lot of stuff to the surface that has been dormant in my body. I will feel this spaciousness in my body right after I do it, and then shortly after that, my body will start screaming at me. All of the tension that was hidden away has been unleashed and is demanding my attention. My hips ache to be opened even more. Knots along my spine will call out to me, screaming at me to go deeper. It's fucking annoying. Getting back on the mat and digging into the tension after time away can be both blissful and painful. But it is worth it. And that is what your F the *shoulds* journey may look like.

At some points it will feel like pure bliss as you allow and claim your **wants**. At other points it may be painful as you dig in and get real with what you have been thinking, believing, and choosing. *Shoulds* can often feel like the easy way out because when you shift to **want**, you have to really face yourself. And that may feel more painful than blissful, but trust me the bliss will come.

Living a life of no *shoulds* takes daily commitment. But it is so fucking worth it. You are worth it. Your **wants** are worth it.

You living *your* life is worth it.

The idea of this book is simple, right? It's all focused around one word, *should*. But as I am guessing you have figured out, while the concept is simple, the work is deep and ongoing. I wish that this book was like *should* repellant—if you have read the book, *shoulds* can't bite you. Unfortunately, it's not. F'ing the *shoulds* is a lifelong daily practice, and it is all up to you. It's just like practicing yoga is for me—some days it may feel easy and some days not, but I always feel the benefits of it. And no matter how long I have been practicing and how often I show up on my mat, that remains true!

The *shoulds* won't go away quietly, and they won't stay away, no matter how seasoned you are at kicking them the F out. **It is up to you to keep coming back to you. To face yourself over and over again and set yourself free over and over again. To trust yourself. To choose yourself. To validate yourself. To allow yourself to see and claim your wants.**

You may forget, you may get lost in some invisible *shoulds,* you may get sucked into the external validation cycle—it happens. But you can always remember; you can always come back to you. Please don't shame yourself or blame yourself. Show yourself love. Show yourself compassion. Show yourself forgiveness.

This life *is yours*. Make it so every day by kicking out the *shoulds* and getting clear on who you are, what *you* **want**, and why you **want** it. Allow yourself to choose it and own it.

F the *shoulds*. Do the wants.

xoxo, Tricia

ACKNOWLEDGMENTS

First of all, thank you for reading this, for opening your heart and mind to this book and to me. For evaluating the *shoulds* in your life and giving yourself the chance to do your **wants**. I truly hope even just one excerpt has supported you.

I am so grateful for all of my life experiences and the people they have involved. Even though the hardships have sucked, yes, I am grateful (in hindsight) for those too, as they have obviously shaped me.

Thank you to my friends of current life and all my past lives, from childhood, to high school, to Columbia College, to House of Blues Chicago, to Sound Image, and all the tour families and friendships created every step of the way.

Thank you to every client and podcast guest who has said yes and inspired me with your honesty and your life stories which have empowered me to keep sharing mine.

Thank you to every person who has supported me over the years, from reading my blogs, sharing social media posts, to buying my products and app, to listening to my podcast and making me feel seen and heard. Thank you Jason for the years of collaboration, support, and friendship. Thank you Amber for being with me from the start and collaborating with me to bring so many creative dreams into fruition with your heart and talent.

Thank you to all those who had a hand, ear, heart in this book. I said over 10 years ago that I was writing a book and kept putting it on the back burner. I have had so many conversations with friends since then who have supported me, cheered me on, and held space for me along the way. A special shout out to my agent, Coleen O'Shea, and to Richelle Fredson and Kristen McGuiness for helping me shape and create my proposal. Thank you Melody Guy and everyone behind the scenes at Hay House who had a hand or even a fingerprint in this book becoming a reality and allowing me to write the book that I wanted to write in my own colorful words.

Thank you Robyn, Tristan, Chaska, Jason, Jess, Kat, Sophie, Stevvi, and Tina for being there for me to vent throughout this process and beyond. Thank you to my family and all the friends that I think of as my family. Thank you to the Mranch for always being a safe place for me to land, heal, and grow.

Zia and Arrow—I hope when you grow up and learn to read that you will WANT to read this book and take your momma's words to heart. I love you more than I can express. Live your wants. I can't wait to see where they will lead you.

ABOUT THE AUTHOR

Tricia Huffman is a podcast host, speaker, Manager of Integrity to Grammy Award-winning artists and founder of Your Joyologist. While living out her first dream as a touring sound engineer, she saw that everyone, including the people we think 'have it all', often don't feel fulfilled and fight doubts, worries and compare themselves to others daily. With her unique background and knowledge in self-care and wellness, she first created her Joyology to keep artists healthy, grounded and inspired in body and mind while on tour. She now spreads her mission to claim joy daily via her empowering social media posts, real talk podcast, coaching work, product line, and Own Your Awesome daily inspiration app.

She is based in Los Angeles, where she is raising her strong-willed, independent, creative daughters and F-ing the *shoulds* while claiming joy daily.

You can learn more about Tricia and her work at triciahuffman.com, @_triciahuffman, yourjoyologist.com, @yourjoyologist and subscribe to her Claim It! podcast.

Hay House Titles of Related Interest

Hay House Podcasts
Bring Fresh, Free Inspiration Each Week!

Hay House proudly offers a selection of life-changing audio content via our most popular podcasts!

Hay House Meditations Podcast

Features your favorite Hay House authors guiding you through meditations designed to help you relax and rejuvenate. Take their words into your soul and cruise through the week!

Dr. Wayne W. Dyer Podcast

Discover the timeless wisdom of Dr. Wayne W. Dyer, world-renowned spiritual teacher and affectionately known as "the father of motivation." Each week brings some of the best selections from the 10-year span of Dr. Dyer's talk show on Hay House Radio.

Hay House Podcast

Enjoy a selection of insightful and inspiring lectures from Hay House Live events, listen to some of the best moments from previous Hay House Radio episodes, and tune in for exclusive interviews and behind-the-scenes audio segments featuring leading experts in the fields of alternative health, self-development, intuitive medicine, success, and more! Get motivated to live your best life possible by subscribing to the free Hay House Podcast.

Find Hay House podcasts on iTunes, or visit
www.HayHouse.com/podcasts for more info.

CONNECT WITH
HAY HOUSE
ONLINE

🌐 hayhouse.co.uk   **f** @hayhouse

📷 @hayhouseuk   🐦 @hayhouseuk

▶ @hayhouseuk   ♪ @hayhouseuk

'The gateways to wisdom and knowledge are always open.'

Louise Hay